KNITTING MEMORIES

REFLECTIONS ON THE KNITTER'S LIFE

KNITTING MEMORIES

REFLECTIONS ON THE KNITTER'S LIFE

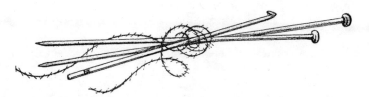

Edited by Lela Nargi

Voyageur Press

Knitting memories: reflections on the knitter's life/edited by Lela Nargi.
    p. cm.
  Includes bibliographical references.
  ISBN-13: 978-0-7603-2648-0
  ISBN-10: 0-7603-2648-7
  1. Knitting. 2. Knitters (Persons)—United States. I. Nargi, Lela.
  TT820.K6998 2006
  746.43'2—dc22

Project Editor: Kari Cornell
Designer: LeAnn Kuhlmann
Printed in China

As ever, for my adoring, adorable family:
Robbie, Ada, Mom, Jaffa, Sigi

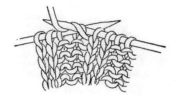

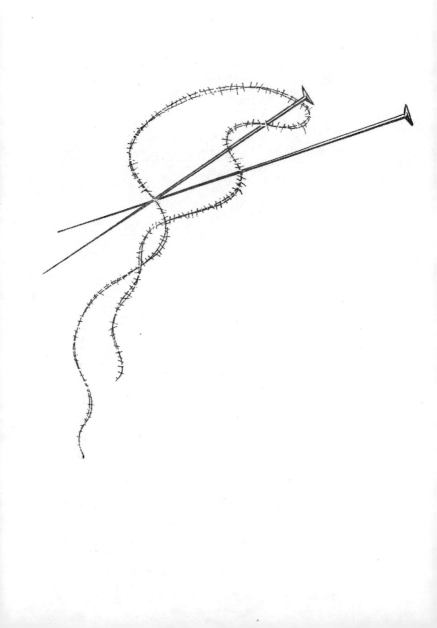

ACKNOWLEDGMENTS

As is the case with all the most fortuitous circumstances of my life, I stumbled into the world of knitting completely by accident. One "accident" led to another, and here I am, at the helm of a second book about knitting, dazed to realize that this miraculous, generous world continues to sustain me in ways both practical and ephemeral. It is impossible to say where this generosity begins, and it certainly seems to have no end. But here I will start by thanking Kari Cornell and the editors at Voyageur Press for taking on this project with unflagging enthusiasm. And go on to thank all the knitters and non-knitters—old friends and new—who practically donated their exquisite writings and drawings to this project. And conclude, at least for the moment, by thanking the wide universe of knitting, for creating a small niche in which I can live and write and knit and be happy.

Contents

INTRODUCTION

From the time she was very, very small, just beginning to form words and steps, my daughter, Ada, has possessed the curious ability to recognize the hand-knit bits and garments strewn throughout our household. With no conscious cues from her knit-loving mother, she is, nevertheless, drawn to them. No, more than drawn to them, fiercely determined to have these things near—around her, over her, under her head—as though their fibers and her own were made of the same stuff.

The first such object of her infatuation was a variegated sweater made for her as a newborn. For over a year, she insisted on being stuffed into this sweater until it held her arms and belly as tightly as sausage casing. If ever I tried to dress Ada in another, she shrieked and flailed, then fell limp in a useless deadweight. I stopped trying. It was (is—a plush penguin wears it now) a beautiful sweater. Soft gradations of pink and lavender and pale green are topped with a lettuce-leaf collar; antique oval mother-of-pearl buttons punctuate the front; a bit of moss stitch peppers each border. But what does a toddler know or see of such details?

At night, as I tuck her in for sleep, she calls off her unvarying list of items she must have surrounding her, in addition to all the usual bedding: "pillow!", a small rectangle topped with an angora and mohair splotch that was my first-ever attempt at knitting; "pink blanket!", really a pink and yellow patchwork of flowers and trees and fanciful foliage ringed by a tasseled border, made by a doting auntie; "blue blanket!", the work of another auntie, patterned with alternating stripes of cream and midnight and light blue. When all have been gathered and arranged, Ada appears as a plumped and wildly uncomfortable miniature maharani, crookedly half-leaning against a tall stack of pillows, sweating beneath one down comforter and a slathering of wool blankets. Under penalty of gruesome toddler meltdown, everything has been painstakingly ordered with no wrinkles, no gaps, tassels just so.

Two years old at this writing, Ada is now tall enough and dexterous enough to open and rummage through dressers, cabinets, armoires. She has managed to unearth a little vest—still too large for her—knitted by some Italian friends. Among the stacks of sweaters and shirts and onesies and pants and skirts and tights, Ada espied this garment, yanked it out, and has begun using it to tuck a favorite doll into a miniature stroller. It is a somewhat unremarkable piece, comprising two white and magenta striped panels knitted flat and stitched together. I try to fathom what about this vest has caught Ada's attention. Does she remember our Italian friends from the time we spent in their company almost a year ago, remember them measuring and plotting and finally finishing this vest with droplets of crochet? I doubt it, and yet . . . who knows? It seems more likely, though, as was the case with her beloved pink sweater, that she somehow recognizes this garment as something handmade and made with her in mind. In the evening, sitting up on the couch in front of a favorite movie and munching a snack, Ada suddenly demands that her "little blanket," as she's taken to calling this simple rectangle she has yet to wear, be brought to her. I retrieve it from the stroller to tuck around her legs. As she alternately watches and munches, Ada takes a second or two to retuck the vest just so, to smooth its edges, stroke its contours.

Admittedly, there are a lot of knitted things in our house. With the enthusiastic input of dozens of knitters around the country, I wrote a book about knitting shortly before I became pregnant with Ada, and when she was born, knitted gifts abounded. This may play some small part in her ability to recognize knitting. But there are many other kinds of handmade things in our house: paintings by Ada's father and numerous friends hang on the walls; curious little assemblages top tables and are tucked into shelves; Ada's ancestors built some of our furniture; I've sewn the curtains. What is it about the knitted things so particularly that calls to her?

Hazarding a simpleton's guess, I'd say that it has to do with the fact that they are eminently tactile and that she is allowed to touch these things (unlike the paintings) and to wear them (unlike the curtains). Some of them have bits she can twiddle and twist, and she can stick her fingers between the stitches. They are soft, fuzzy, bright. But as I've indicated, many of them have also been knitted just for her, by people who know and love her. Perhaps a whiff of this cherishing perfumes the fabric. This notion is whimsical, as notions go, and yet it does not strike me as outlandish. Knitting, somehow—powerfully—has permeated Ada's consciousness. At the age of two she lives already with a strong, almost Proustian sense of it. Maybe it's just genetic.

This past winter, as I sat gazing in awe, for the umpteenth time, at a blanket knitted by my friend Elanor, I was finally moved to write about it. The piece, "Living with Elanor," is the first in the collection gathered here. And as soon as I had finished writing about the blanket and my relationship to it, I thought, "Isn't it so with all of us who live with knitting?" This blanket of Elanor's, and these pieces of knitting that Ada is drawn to, are intricate stories waiting to be unraveled, and mostly they are stories about relationships. Between knitter and knitting—and by this I mean not only the tangible knitted thing itself (sweater, blanket, hat), but also the very personal and subjective act of knitting. Between knitter and the person he knits for, even if that person is himself. Between the person who has received a piece of knitting, whatever the circumstances, and this object she adores. The story can be one that has to do with history, tracing knitting's broad and narrow channels though the ages, linking knitters to ancient craftspeople or perhaps just our own mothers and grand-mothers. And the story is also, sometimes, one about pure imagination—the way knitting exists in our minds as fertile territory to be plumbed, picked at, reveled in, and perhaps eventually presented to others so that they, too, may share in the imaginings.

This book tells of sixteen such relationships. Throughout its pages are essays by knitters (and also who I'll call "experiencers" of knitting) such as designers Lily Chin, who writes about knitting for a living; Teva Durham, writing about the oddity of knitting-world celebrity; and Kathryn Alexander, on co-existing with an ancestral collec-tion of ski sweaters. North Dakota photographer (and non-knitter) Cedric N. Chatterly lays bare a deep association with a luckless knitter and her son. Hospice-care nurse Veda Alban writes about knitting through the death of her mother, and Reine Wing Hewitt about knitting through and around bouts of manic depression. Writers Betty Christiansen and Clara Parkes, respectively, muse about "chestnuts"—those old, never worn pieces that clutter our attics and that we cling to nevertheless—and living with various and peculiar knitting-related afflictions ("yarnilepsy," "yarnitopia"). And Elanor Lynn, the eponymous Elanor of much of my writing about knitting, gives a glimpse into her complex, often fantastical creative universe.

It is no secret, no surprise to knitters that knitting resonates in the lives of all sorts of people. Herein lie just a handful of stories about the art, the craft, the dream that binds us together.

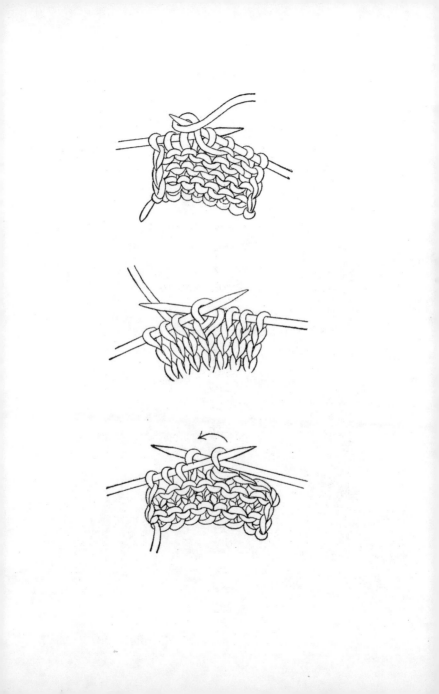

Illustration by Lela Nargi

LIVING WITH ELANOR

by Lela Nargi

I've won precisely two things in my life. The first was a giant stuffed frog, seagreen in color and grinning widely across its broad face with a look bordering on lecherous. I won it for my Halloween unicorn costume at a church contest in 1975, a brief episode in which I cantered around a gymnasium in my patent-leather Mary Janes, a white felt tunic, and a gold spray-painted horn assembled from rolled cardboard and a spiral of twine. As I recall, this costume of mine—conceived by me and constructed by my mother— was voted "most unusual" by the church's panel of Halloween judges. I can't remember my competition, no doubt having shuttered my mind against its inevitable superhero blandness.

Sorry to say, the frog trophy was thoroughly unbeloved— something about that look—and a sad commentary on the state of my luck for some twenty-five years to follow. Three years ago, though, I won something much more estimable. Although I was initially thrilled as much as startled by this winning, the true extent of its significance has only begun to sink in, as I've had the chance to live with it.

The "it" in question is a blanket made by my friend Elanor. Elanor is a talented, imaginative, and prolific knitter. I've lived with other of her creations—most recently, another, smaller blanket she knit when my daughter was born and a host of whimsical sweaters. But there is something more to this victory blanket, as I'll call it, something that pulls it away from the realm of merely exceptional knitting, or rather, pulls me in, to its own subtext, which is of course intimately linked to Elanor's brain.

Perhaps this has to do with the blanket's background. It was created with a purpose: Elanor's fiancé was laid off from work and suddenly found himself in need of dental surgery he could not afford. As a secret undertaking to raise the funds, Elanor constructed this blanket and raffled it off among his friends. I'm not sure how many weeks she worked at it. But I do know that she knitted swatches of it day after day whenever she had a moment: walking across the Williamsburg Bridge into Manhattan, riding the subway, chatting on the phone while soup percolated on the stove and a cup of strong tea grew cold in its thin Majolica cup on the ottoman. I can picture her. Her eyeglasses are pushed up firmly to the top of her nose and her coral-colored lips are set. Needles fly—the wood ones she inherited from a friend's grandmother or the celluloid ones that were given to her as a girl by one of her early knitting mentors. Elanor hurries, but in a way she enjoys and that becomes her; in her best moments, she seems to buzz just above the surface of the couch cushions in a state of happy fluster. Now and then, she consults a stitch pattern in a Barbara Walker book; more often she improvises. Time evaporates.

The result of this engrossment is about fifty swatches in myriad colors, disparate sizes, and seemingly incompatible shapes, ingeniously lashed together to form a perfect rectangle. Within the blanket's double border of knitted stripes and several rows of nonchalant crochet huddles a jumble of imagery: a tiny goldfish; a funnel filled with snake-headed grasses; a pair of trees à la van Gogh, bare branches vivid against a stubbled landscape; a peach; a canoe-shaped bit of blue and green; a purple-hearted sunflower whose ruffle of petals tickle my chin at night as I sleep.

Elanor delivered the blanket to me on a hot afternoon, arriving at my door with the thing wrapped about her like a bulbous cape. She extricated herself then abruptly left my apartment; I realize now she probably couldn't bear the parting. Thus, the ensuing ceremony for the victory blanket was all mine. I gave in to a pang of thrill at my winning, tossed the blanket onto my bed and adjusted it just so, then spent the next half hour gazing at its panels. I tallied what I saw, delighting in recognition: apple trees, a square of raisin stitch; an ochre-rimmed eye, the profile of a sweet gray bunny, and was that a Japanese fighting fish? What I didn't recognize I chalked up to whimsy, and I assumed the squares of no particular pattern were born of an attempt to use up the dregs of a yarn stash. No matter; the victory blanket, contemplated in its entirety, was a gorgeous thing. I was excited every night to drape it over me—even in the ensuing summer swelter—and to call it mine.

Sometime in July Elanor called. She wanted to come over and visit the blanket, maybe take its picture. She would call a number of times over the months, wanting to borrow the blanket for various reasons, all of which annoyed me. After all, I'd won this blanket fair and square, and it was mine now, and I didn't want to part with it. But on this first visit to the victory blanket, Elanor asked me, "So, have you figured out what all the swatches are?" Something in her tone—a giddy tremor—made me catch myself before I began to rattle off the list of fishes and flowers I'd compiled. And, struck with a split second of dread—I thought I knew this blanket—I said, "Um, what do you mean?"

"Oh well," said Elanor, pausing to draw a meaningful breath. "I don't want to ruin anything for you." With these words I knew I was going to have to reconsider every inch of the blanket. "So I'll just tell you that one of the swatches was inspired by this photograph I saw in a magazine of Red Buttons's swimming pool."

Red Buttons's swimming pool? I stopped a moment to scan the blanket in my mind's eye. "You mean the blue and ochre eyeball?" I asked, feeling a bit light-headed.

"That's right!" said Elanor, sounding as delighted as a nursery-school teacher at some obvious pronouncement made by one of her charges. "I can't wait to hear what you think the rest of the swatches are."

"Hah, hah, yes," I said weakly. I didn't know how to tell her that if she was knitting up interpretations of Red Buttons's swimming pool, there was no way I'd ever hit upon the meaning of the small square with a blotch like a chicken liver in the center of it. Or the red patch with the limey jag, which I'd thought was one of those end-of-skeins undertakings. Really, even the true connotation of the peach, and the apple trees, and the simple patch of raisin stitch, now seemed to require excavation.

There was nothing to do but have at it. Instead of gazing fondly and knowingly at the victory blanket as I tucked myself in, I took to climbing into bed before I was tired in order to contemplate its intricacies. For a while, I was certain I could crack the blanket, like you might crack a code, one piece falling into place and the rest yielding thereafter in an exhilarating domino effect. Red Buttons's swimming pool was solved (okay, donated). Onward.

The next swatch to give was the giant frog. Clearly, a symbol of Elanor herself. She's had a passion for frogs as long as I've known her; she wears a gold frog ring on the ring finger of her left hand, an engagement present from her fiancé, and frogs decorate many of the things she makes, as her trademark. Several days later, I decided that the bunny must be the fiancé. I had almost nothing on which to base this assumption, only a giddy memory of him in a bunny "costume" that consisted of little more than a scowl and a pair of enormous, puffy rabbit ears Elanor had knitted for him. Feeling rather pleased with myself, I reckoned that with three pieces solved in four or five days, I should have the entire blanket decoded by around Christmas.

But from then on, nothing. I studied and wracked my brains and tried to recollect every quirk of Elanor's personality—some twenty years' worth of information. After the bunny, not a single panel of the victory blanket budged. There has been not one breakthrough in almost three years. So, resorting to a whimsy of my own, I've begun concocting small stories to accompany each image. The Japanese fighting fish is a metaphor for the Elanor's "vision quest" beneath the cherry blossoms at the Brooklyn Botanic Garden shortly before she began studying karate. She took a roll of strange, hilarious, but breathtakingly beautiful Polaroids of this near-solitary event: a Bruce Lee figurine/companion/spiritual guide poised on a branch before a hazy backdrop of koi pond and weeping willow;

wielding a sprig of pine needles; meditating atop a bed of pale pink petals; posed as though ready to deliver a mighty wallop to the side of Elanor's head.

The greenish chicken-liver-y splotch must symbolize Elanor's repulsion for meat. She's been a vegetarian all her life, and although she has on occasion mustered the courage to muscle a piece of steak into the broiler for her fiancé, it is with obvious relief that she returns her culinary attentions to her vegetable potages and pungent cheeses. The patch of raisin stitch represents some healthful but delicious tartlet her mother made for her eighth birthday—this "observation" is 100 percent fabrication on my part; I haven't met her mother and have never known Elanor to speak of a single birthday from her childhood. But when fact fails, fantasy comes to the fore.

In its own subtly acquiescent way, the blanket yields, now and then, to my imaginings. Every day I look at it and think about it. And every day I think of Elanor, even though we haven't spoken for months and the blanket and I no longer live within visiting distance of her. I'm sorry for this. I know now what I didn't know at the time of winning, which is that the blanket is as much a part of Elanor as her fingers that knitted it. When she visited or borrowed the blanket, she was, in a very real sense, checking in with a piece of herself. To see the blanket again was to relive moments of her history, expressed through the conjuring of artifacts from bits and bolts of yarn. And it was a way to tap in to a wellspring of sentiment, not only for certain occurrences in her past, but also for her present life with her fiancé, whose circumstances compelled her to knit the blanket in the first place.

As for me, to be able to think of Elanor every day, whether I summon her through fact or fiction, is a luxury. Like every working mother I know, I am busy. In my few toddler-free hours a day, I scramble to send e-mails, pay bills, make phone calls, shower, eat, tidy up, all this before I even get to my real work of writing. There is so little time to lavish thoughts on anyone beyond myself and my most immediate family. In such a climate, even the sturdiest friendships lag and fizzle. This can be lonely, and more than a little depressing. But for three years now, with the victory blanket as an unexpected psychic connector, I have had the pleasure of living with Elanor. Through its intricate, mysterious weavings I can pretend, when I can't check in by e-mail or phone, to know what it is that Elanor is thinking, and what it is that makes her tick, and knit.

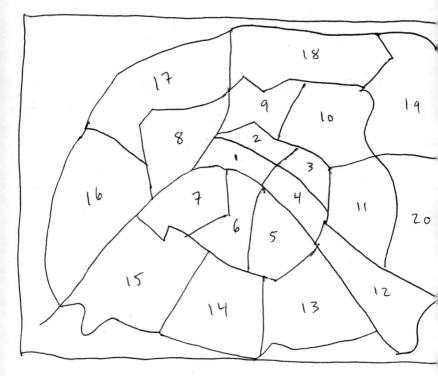

Illustration by Elanor Lynn

PARIS CHARM BLANKET

by Elanor Lynn

"What is a cell?" I asked my maternal grandfather, Stuart Grinnell, a professor of
chemistry at Stanford University. It was
1974, and I had learned to knit earlier that year, as a sixth-
birthday present from his daughter, my mother, Anne.

"Would you like the sentence version, the paragraph
version, or the chapter version?"

"Sentence, please."

"A cell is the basic unit of life."

My grandfather was just as likely to have answered by
consulting Webster's Third Edition, and quoting this
excerpt from the first entry, sense 5: "the least structural
aggregate of living matter capable of functioning as an
independent unit." Fluent in ancient Greek and Latin,
Stuart spent his retirement rereading the classics, punctuated by periodic doses of Scientific American. He
never patronized me, and he could answer any question

encyclopedically. His curiosity cabinet included authentic moon rocks, furniture-sized handmade cameras, World War II ration stamps, teeth, bones, and skins. One day, he put an ancient Peruvian textile fragment in my hands.

"This was woven circa 26,000 B.C."

Perhaps, thanks to genetics and the happy times I spent with my grandfather combined with my incurable curiosity about everything, I consider myself a scientist of knitting. "What happens if?" is the question that drives me every day to find new ways to describe what I see through the structure of needle arts. My formal education was unconventional, and science was not included in the curriculum. This lack of training, along with my genuine inquisitiveness, fostered the development of my knitting methodology, which is based on the conviction that there are no mistakes, only design opportunities. That is, there is no accident that cannot also function as a pattern element in another context. Let me quote my knitting hero, Elizabeth Zimmerman, from her revolutionary 1971 manifesto, Knitting Without Tears: "Show me a 'mistake' and I will show you that it is only a misplaced pattern or inappropriate technique." For example, lace patterns are based on a yarn-over (which makes a hole and a new stitch) paired with a decrease to balance the new stitch made by the yarn-over hole. Unfortunately, when that same yarn-over is made spontaneously by a new knitter, it is usually called an error.

Through experimentation with the arrangement of basic elements, endless new patterns and techniques are possible.

I used to focus on dense, complex patterns of texture and color executed in a craft tradition that values "correct" interpretations based upon mathematical precision. Eventually, I found a way to transform the rigidity of my technique and learned to unhomogenize my work by applying an aesthetic that recognizes variation as the foundation of evolution.

My mathematical ability is limited to the basic arithmetic I need to know to solve knitting and sewing problems. Although I cannot express what I do in mathematical terms, I can make complex patterns fit into and relate to the complex curves of sleeve and armhole shaping. How did I learn? Through trial and error. By asking myself, "What works?" and conducting experiments.

Most of the blankets I knit now are crazy quilts. I think of them as communities composed of independent units that come together in an unscripted visual dialogue. For example, each New Year's Day, I collect the year's worth of "compost" (gauge swatches, abandoned projects, experiments, and studies) and recycle the pile into a document that tells a story about what I did during the past year. Because knitting is so completely integrated into my life—I knit every day, often while I am doing other things like sitting with a friend, reading, or walking—

each piece I knit holds memories of and associations with the time and place where it was born. Each piece has its own internal logic, but I don't know how all the pieces will fit together until I've decided there are enough pieces. Sometimes that is determined by when I run out of yarn.

Once the pile of pieces is big enough, I sweep and mop my kitchen floor, lay out the pieces, and play with the puzzle for an hour or so, until it works. At the beginning of assembly, I crochet many units together because I like the raised ridge it makes, a sharp line marrying the odd shapes. I work quickly, as if I were painting a fresco into wet plaster, because I have to complete the assembly in one day. Otherwise, I might get distracted by other projects and delay finishing indefinitely. By afternoon, I start using another method, the faster overcast or whipstitch, to connect units. There will still be a border to knit (often elaborate) and zillions of loose ends of yarn, hanging like an all-over fringe on the reverse side to weave in (always tedious), but I finish assembling the composition before I sleep.

Unlike most of the blankets I make, the following story of the Paris Charm Blanket represents several departures from my usual methods. First, it is not a crazy quilt; each unit was planned and executed in precise order. Second, it is not composed of scraps; each unit is created for the sole purpose of being a cell in my painting. Third, I won't ever give it away; it is a present to myself.

OBJECTIVE: LEARN THE NAMES OF
THE ARRONDISSEMENTS OF PARIS

"Arrondissement" comes from the verb "arrondir," to make round, or the action of making round. To haul in Webster's Third again, it is "a ward or administrative district of some large cities of France <Paris is subdivided into twenty.>" As cells are the smallest unit of life, arrondissements are the largest units of life in Paris. From a bird's eye view, the arrondissements form a logarithmic spiral of Parisian neighborhoods, whirling out from the center.

Louvre, Bourse, Temple, Hôtel de Ville, Panthéon, Luxembourg, Palais Bourbon, Élysée, Opéra, Enclos Saint Laurent, Popincourt, Reuilly, Gobelins, Observatoir, Vaugirard, Passy, Batignolles, Butte Montmartre, Buttes Chaumont, Ménilmontant. From first to twentieth, these are the names of the arrondissements as they are written on the 1960s Paris subway map I bought on the street for five dollars this past spring. This map is not the only version of the arrondissements. Earlier versions, with different names and varied configurations, as well as later modifications, exist in abundance.

At the time I bought the Map, a possible trip to Paris had been in my mind for years. When I found the Map, I knew I had received a postcard from my future. I was instantly struck by the arrangement of the arrondissements, by the way they spiral counter-clockwise out from the center. Had I never looked at a map of Paris before? Simply, no. But once I saw the structure of Paris, I became obsessed with learning the names of the arrondissements, as they appear on the Map. The contemporary practice of calling the neighborhoods by their ordinals (i.e., "the seventeenth") has apparently caused these names to become virtually extinct. It occurred to me that knitting a map of the city would be an easy and delightful way to learn the names of the arrondissements, become familiar with the geography of the city, and keep the names alive a little longer.

For many years, I dreamt of visiting Paris. My reluctance to go was due to a fear of spoiling the Paris I had imagined, assembled from a lifetime of watching movies, looking at photographs, and listening to rumors of café life. My Paris was composed primarily of images from such sources as films like Children of Paradise, L'Atalante, Jules and Jim, and Gigi; and photographs by Atget and Brassai. Collectively, these images formed an a-historic, impossible city in my mind.

In June, after years of dreaming, Sean and I finally decided to go. This would be Sean's first trip back since he lived in Paris between 1988 and 1989. Having the opportunity to be introduced to Sean's Paris took the edge off my fear of losing the pristine Paris of my imagination. As a common-law couple, would this trip be an unofficial honeymoon? Would that make the blanket part of my trousseau?

PREPARATION

Two weeks before we left, fueled by a quart of Red Bull drunk during a day of preparing real estate contracts at my law office, I came home and parked myself in front of the Map, which I'd hung on the wall of my six-by-six-feet windowless studio/closet. Perched at the edge of my desk, I frantically drew, sketched, and measured until 4:00 A.M., until I had completed architectural crib notes on each arrondissement. These hastily worked diagrams were all I planned to consult during knitting. In truth, though, I cheated and stole many glances at the Map, often aided by a ruler.

In theater, there is a truism that one must not over-rehearse, the goal being to arrive at opening night prepared, fresh, able to continue the process of development before routine sets in. In that spirit, I wanted to work from purposefully inadequate sketches to force/trick myself into straying from an exact replica. I improvised by exploiting external factors, such as when my train arrived at First Avenue to inform the shaping of the pieces, rather than relying solely on what I thought was correct. Running out of yarn or picking my work up after a pause were other circumstances that functioned as design elements. I looked for opportunities to disrupt the process of thinking.

It was exhilarating to make work so far off the grid that I got lost.

As I started to knit, the work suddenly took on an absurd, imperative importance, and I knitted like mad. Our departure date approached, and I increased my pace, determined to complete each of the arrondissements prior to my arrival, as if they would not be there waiting for me if I hadn't first knit them into existence.

MATERIALS

I purposefully underbought yarn, partially to economize but mostly because I knew interesting things would happen if I ran out of yarn and had to cobble bits together to complete some sections. While I briefly flirted with the idea of other palettes, I decided to stick to the colors of the Map: yellow, blue, pink, and orange. Typically, I favor strong colors, especially greens and reds. Back from the yarn store, I laid out my stash and recoiled from the pile of pastels. Yet I resolved to submit my will to the will of my palette; I would make it work. As this was to be a summer blanket, I chose to work primarily with cotton, with some linen, silk, and merino wool thrown in to supply contrast in texture.

CONSTRUCTION

Perpetually phobic of boredom, I briefly considered making each section in a different stitch pattern. Fortunately, I rejected that idea as an invitation to insanity and settled on garter stitch, which has a superior ability to mush and stretch as needed. Having assembled dozens of scrap blankets and crazy quilts, I have learned that unlikely shapes, of any stitch or pattern, can be made to fit together. Bolstered by this knowledge, I proceeded with the project. As an explorer, I enjoyed the prospect of embarking with my insufficient information and was curious to find out what would happen.

I worked the arrondissements in a variety of yarn weights, on various needle sizes, increasing and decreasing stitches as needed. I also exploited change of gauge as a shaping device, in place of increasing and decreasing. Short rows, a technique where you turn the work around in the middle of a row, allowed me to improvise shaping by progressively building up one side higher than the other.

I knit during every moment not spent sleeping or at the office, in order to stay on pace in this imaginary tour of Paris. I completed each section of the blanket in order—Louvre, Bourse, and so on. On the day we left for Paris, I had knitted half the basic structure of the Buttes Chaumont (the nineteenth), up to where the Parc des Buttes-Chaumont would go. On this trip to Paris, we would not visit it. And so, I thought, when I eventually embroidered its place on the blanket, I would also be embroidering my imagination of it, thus prolonging my delight in reaching it one day.

NOT KNITTING IN PARIS: MY FIRST DAY

We arrived at 6:00 A.M. at Charles de Gaulle airport, took a bus into the city via Butte Montmartre (the eighteenth); arrived at the edge of Opéra and Bourse (the nineth and the second); walked through the manicured, dusty Tuileries garden in Louvre (the first); crossed the glistening Seine at the bridge, Pont Royal; arrived on the Left Bank, at Palais Bourbon (the seventh); and continued to Rue du Bac, admiring the shops on our way to number ninety-three, where we woke our sleeping host. After walking for nearly three kilometers, I began to assemble a sense of the scale of the city. Sean had always told me how small and walkable the city was—I'd imagined it to be about the size of Manhattan below Fourteenth Street.

Our temporary home was elegant enough for a movie star—it lacked only a balcony. The interior windows opened onto a five-floor view of a classic Parisian courtyard; the exterior windows opened onto a view of a neighbor's beaux-arts garden, framed by a towering diorama of eighteenth- and nineteenth-century buildings that looked as if they had been borrowed from a movie set. The phrase "the chimney pots of Paris" floated unattributably through my head as I gazed across the rooftops. Each rooftop was dusted, fungi-like, with hand-thrown red clay pots. I wondered if they would be full of smoke in November. For five days, we would wake to this view, our view. With so glorious a home, it often took us until the afternoon to venture out.

The apartment had history. We learned from the housekeeper that the odd tilt to our doorway, on the fifth floor landing, had been made by a Prussian cannonball in the 1870s. I worried about ghosts. But this furnished rental was subject only to another form of haunting: daily surprise tours by prospective tenants and their agents. Other than that minor flaw, it was perfect, the kind of place where even Parisians dream about living.

That first morning, while Callum, our Scottish host and a former Brooklyn neighbor, consumed his morning ration of forty-three e-mails, twenty-seven phone calls, and a half-dozen espressos, Sean and I were content to have a post-red-eye sprawl on the overstuffed couches and admire the view across the courtyard of window pots containing lavender, geranium, and herbs. Later, when we headed out for a stroll, we made it only about three blocks before stopping at a bistro on Rue de Grenelle for "elevenses" of Leff, a light Belgian beer with a refreshing, hoppey tooth. Thus reinforced, we made our way further east past the Boulevard Raspail and into Luxembourg (the sixth), where, after some light window shopping we were again obliged to make a pit stop for more Leff, this time fortified with sandwiches and salad, at Café Palette on

Rue de Seine. We tucked into a bushy, shady corner and squeaked on wicker seats among locals having a usual day. The legend of Parisian chic is true: coming from informal Brooklyn, it was strange to be surrounded by elegant women. The baguette cliché is true too: at noon and 5:00 P.M., it seems everyone is carrying a baguette under their arm or has one tucked into their knapsack as they bicycle by.

With so many cafés to choose from, I was grateful to be guided by Callum. On my own, I might wander for hours, looking at every one before making my selection—in a town full of cafes as unique as the people they contain, there are many right choices. Café Palette, situated in a fashionable pedestrian shopping district, made for ideal people watching. While I imagined spending an entire afternoon or even a series of afternoons here, scrawling in notebooks, reading, and observing, Callum took several more phone calls. Then he announced we were going to St. Chappelle, a mid-thirteenth-century chapel in the oldest part of the city, on the Ile de la Cité, in the shadow of Notre Dame. It is famous for a lofty upper chapel featuring stained-glass windows that depict the history of mankind as told by the Bible. Except for Eiffel's tower, at the foot of which we ate Roserie Grenelle's radishes dipped in Barthelemy's salt, the chapel was to be the only tourist attraction we saw.

After having spent twenty minutes in line waiting to enter, I was shocked that Sean and Callum were ready to leave St. Chappelle after only ten minutes. I accepted the challenge of absorbing the chapel's lifetime worth of image, texture, and pattern, all dramatically illuminated by one bright June day, in the three extra minutes I negotiated. At that moment, about seven hours into my trip, I understood that no amount of time would be enough to absorb all of Paris. For the next five days, rather than focus on all that I could not see, I decided to relax and enjoy what came to me.

We headed home so that our host could get ready to go to work for the afternoon. We passed through the central courtyard of the Louvre and made our way for the second time that day to the garden Callum calls the "Twilleries." Enjoying a cone of coffee ice cream, I stumbled down a few steps as we descended into the garden. I caught my fall with my left knee and left hand. Paris bit me. Later that evening, one of Callum's buddies, Eva, explained why I must allow Paris to change me: it's going to anyway, so just let it. I couldn't know what she meant yet; I understood that I would change, but not how.

Knitting usually occupies from one to three hours of my day, occasionally peaking at up to eleven or more hours. Five to seven hours is not unusual for me, especially when under deadline. I did not knit once during my entire stay in Paris. I wanted my first immersion in Paris to be free from the pressure to produce so that I could concentrate on consuming. Like a smoker trying to quit, I packed an emergency skein and needles, just in case. Thus armed, I went with the plan to not knit and managed to succeed.

ASSEMBLY

In the two weeks leading up to our trip, as each piece of the blanket was completed, it joined its numerical counterparts on the kitchen floor, where my cats graced the tableau with their sprawls and fur, constantly disturbing the arrangement. It became a pseudo-rug that we continued to live with for many weeks upon our return from Paris.

At this point, my fear of completing the blanket became so paralyzing that I took the luxury of a month to languish over the knitting of the final one and a half arrondissements. During this time, I discovered I would have surgery in a few weeks to remove a lump, which would turn out to be benign. My fear of how to assemble this pile of mush into a map resembling Paris functioned as a repository of fear for my health. Where I first tore through the knitting at breakneck speed, hungry to devour Paris, I lingered ever more slowly, drawing out the last stages of knitting, reluctant to finish my meal.

With the twenty pieces finally complete, I had to concede they did not fit. There were overlaps and gaps. Rather than chide myself for failing to make it all fit perfectly on the first try, I relished the opportunity to go back and rework certain sections. A devotee of the composer John Cage, the choreographer Merce Cunningham, and their collaboration, I invite chance methodologies. The opportunity to reknit as a form of mending thrills me. Mending (bricolage) is the highest form of art I know. Using available materials, one fixes that which is broken and makes it go again, and the place where something is mended becomes the strongest part of the structure. I mostly resisted my instinct to refer back to the Map, and worked instead from the relationships of the existing pieces, seeing how each needed to be filled out to fit its neighbor. I picked up stitches at odd angles to emphasize the additions and ripped out where needed. I also used another fiber and shade of the same color, which has the effect of shading, either lighter or darker, at random edges to further emphasize the revisions.

The day before surgery, I finally began assembly. I worked systematically, again from the center of the spiral, not worrying about any other section but the two immediate edges to be joined. I used a fifth color—white, as dictated by the Map—to join the units, using single crochet for the seams, which forms a heavy, raised line, By the morning of my surgery, I had completed most of the Left Bank, grateful to have such an engaging transitional object in which to indulge.

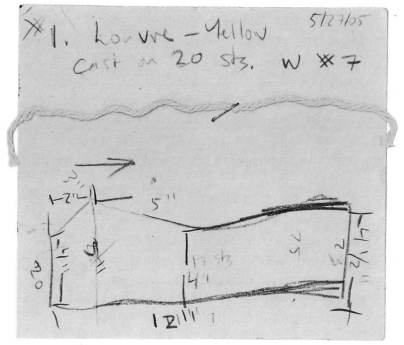

Illustration by Elanor Lynn

It came together all at once, and I completed assembly within a few days.

The two halves of Paris, though, were still separated by the empty strip where the Seine would be. Before knitting it, I first had to confirm that the river flows from right to left so that I could knit it with the current. Next, I chose a 3-mm needle to produce a fine gauge in which to represent the details of how the river meets the land. For yarn, I granted myself a slight departure from my palette of pastels, succumbing to a sparkling medium blue silk-merino blend. I didn't have enough light blue left for the islands so I dyed some cotton kitchen twine to knit on a tight gauge to make the islands stand out from the Seine on all sides. As I knit the long, narrow river (about eighty inches by one inch), I became aware that joining the Right and Left Banks was a metaphor for joining my right and left brains, the improvisational with the choreographic, the Kirk and the Spock. The Seine also represented my suture growing back together, knitting itself together. When completed, my Seine had approximately one thousand rows twisting one thousand times around themselves with each turn. Was it generating energy as it coiled, DNA-like, around itself?

EPILOGUE: THE CHARMS

During the knitting of the blanket, I'd gotten caught up in the idea that I was creating a canvas that would later serve as a background for knitted iconographic charms, each of which would represent an experience, either as I had actually lived it on my first trip to Paris or as I'd planned for future trips. The collection of charms would function as a visual list of things I had done and would do, as well as places I had gone and would go. Additionally, I intended to embroider lines representing each path I traveled on every stroll I took in Paris, creating a densely layered tracing of lines. The Paris Charm Blanket would function as a bracelet upon which to hang the souvenirs of my experience and imagination. For example, on our last evening at our favorite café, the owner doled out oversized white Café Varenne umbrellas to our entire party. Sean and I wound up with three. The spectacle of getting the three umbrellas through customs (which we had to do three times on our way home, thanks to a changeover in Niçe) was hilarious. The symbol of a white umbrella, placed on the blanket where Rue Varenne crosses Rue du Bac, would serve to memorialize both the evenings we spent among friends at the Café Varenne and the comic hassle of dragging the souvenirs home.

But now that I have conceived the knitted umbrella, carrying through with the literal charm seems redundant. And herein lies the most surprising result of assembling the blanket: I find myself as reluctant to create and affix charms to it as I once was to visit the city. For now, at least, I prefer superimposing imagined details onto the blanket's uncluttered surface. Rather than committing to specific charms, I am preserving the possibility of multiple readings. I might still make charms; maybe there will eventually be a grand set of cross-indexed, detachable charms from which I can create infinitely changeable sets. But I don't know—don't want to know—how this story will end yet.

I now realize that the Tuileries' gravel in my hand and knee is a symbol. As rennet curdles cheese, Paris curdled me. Paris taught me to enjoy what is presently before me. While the ability to imagine places and things is an important creative instinct—after all, it allowed me to create the blanket in the first place— it can also be a distraction from experiencing what is directly around you. Parisian bread and butter do live up to all my expectations; but the bread and butter at home in New York are just as wonderful. To the extent that I linger over the memory of that pat of butter on that slice of Poilâne bread on that afternoon in June, I am distracting myself from the charm of what I am now eating.

I took only one roll of photographs in Paris. I could have shot a hundred rolls in those five days, but then the trip would have been about taking photographs. Reviewing the roll at home, I discovered another postcard from Paris. A chipped enamel sign affixed to the side of a building read: "D'EFENSE D'AFFICHER/LOI DU 29 JULLIET 1881." (No posting, by order of Law/29 July 1881.) Though originally intended to thwart communication among dissidents, it serves as the slogan for my new regime. "No posting" means leave it alone. Embellish less.

Since returning from Paris, not only have I resisted adorning the blanket, but I have also been inspired to divest myself of the many trinkets and collections I have acquired in the first half of my life. An avid thriftshopper from the age of ten, I have amassed some stuff. It is time, I now realize, to suss out the treasures and toss the dross. I am content now to leave the blanket plain, as a metaphor for my current life. The arrondissements are the charms in my life, as I actually experienced them, and require no further gilding.

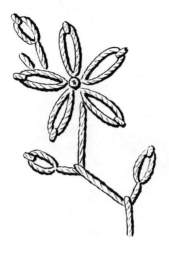

Illustration by Cedric Chatterley

VIRGINIA

by Cedric N. Chatterley

I t was the nineteen-year-old boy who I met first that day. He saw that I held a camera and asked if I worked for the newspaper, but I was just watching the end of a Shriner's parade in a southern Illinois town I hardly knew on the first Saturday of October, 1985. Just another master of fine arts student looking for something to photograph. Behind us his mother called out from the porch steps and asked where I was from and what brought me here. I could not answer the boy and her and the man drinking beer next to her at the same time—his head tilted, also curious—and by now the boy had actually taken me by the arm and spoken directly: Come into our house, I want to show you how we live here, I want you to make pictures of everything that's broken.

We stepped past his mother and the man. Inside the house was made dark by nailed up army blankets for curtains. The boy directed me to leaky bathroom plumbing, cracked window panes in his own tiny bedroom, and a broken back-door lock. I felt like a police detective with a camera and wished for more light.

51

Later, outside, the boy parted his mother's dark hair with his fingers and explained that the fresh, jagged scar was from a street fight two nights earlier. Jumped for no reason, she was, while walking home.

You can't trust anybody, she said.

The boy asked when the pictures would be in the Cairo Evening Citizen. Maybe then the landlord would be forced to fix everything.

The son and his mother now live in a different house, in a different southern Illinois town, not far from where we met twenty years ago. My name is on their painted mailbox just below their names. Most of the letters from both our names have fallen off, but when I pull into the driveway late at night about every two months, I sit and think: According to my driver's license, I am home. This place—their home and my sometimes home—is central to my travels, both real and imagined. It has become the real hub on all my journeys and, likewise, the destination of choice within my imagination when competing memories fail the long list of reasons why memories are kept at all.

Their stories and my story—our lives—weave together like big, loose fabric, or a patchwork blanket, and it is no longer important to know the reasons why the bonds between us are so strong. The details of hardship, kinship, broken spirits, and the son's three young boys being swept away by The System will one day be told in another story. I have become the biographer of these friends of mine, people to whom I am closer in many ways than to my own family. It might take our entire lives for me to tell it all.

Now Virginia sits and knits, and Mark fixes what needs fixing, and when I drive into town I sleep in the room where Mark's boys slept until Mother's Day weekend, 1998. The second boy has my name, the only other Cedric I have ever known. I have not seen him in seven years.

I think Virginia has always knitted, but I don't remember seeing her knit as much as she does now. She recently told me that she learned a good deal from her long-dead aunt. That old woman would use kite string, anything she could find like that.

I asked her why she knits so much, especially now. To me it seems like such a sacrifice, but then she tells me about the new grandchild coming to one of Mark's older sisters, who lives an hour away. Perhaps knitting this blanket will bring the new grandchild closer. Virginia keeps knitting and does not look up. It eases my mind. I don't worry so much or think about things I shouldn't think about. But I stop when my hands go hurting and when they feel better I start up again.

Virginia calls me son.

About three years ago she began giving me knitted scarves, round and floppy table-top doilies and small nap blankets. The yarn is bright yellow, burnt orange, purple, various shades of pale green, some white—but not much—and crimson red. She tells me bright colors make things look better. Right away I'm not sure what to do with these gifts, but Virginia has given them to me and they are mine now. Holding these gifts reminds me that I am sentimental, and when people give me something made by hand, I feel extremely honored. Almost sad, too, I think, but mostly honored. I guess this mixture adds up to sentimental.

The scarf I wear in the winter, but for a long while I didn't know what to do with the doilies because I really don't own any furniture. The small nap blanket covers my camera bag on the passenger seat of my car.

Virginia handed me a hat during a visit early last year. Give this one to your girlfriend. It is sort of floppy, bright purple, with some baby blue trim and strings that tie under the chin. It's old timey, she smiles.

Very late the next day I get out of my car in South Dakota. My girlfriend is very grateful, and surprised by the hat, and I sense in her some of the same feelings I feel when I first hold a gift from Virginia. She pulls the hat over her medium-length blonde hair, holds the strings below her chin but does not tie them, then finds herself in the hallway mirror. She lays the hat on her lap and touches it with her long fingers while we catch up on the past few weeks. The hat is thoughtfully put away the next morning, and she sends a thank-you card on Saturday. I call Mark the following week, and his mother gets on the phone and tells me how nice it was to get the card in the mail.

Months later my girlfriend gives me a bag of yarn. Give this to Virginia when you go down and see her and Mark. I think she might like this yarn. I look in the bag, and the yarn is a delicate mixture of wine and earth colors that would look good on my girlfriend. Soft, dark, and muted.

A few months pass, and we half expect a scarf or maybe a new hat knitted from this yarn. But this does not happen. What I am given during a late-November visit to southern Illinois is more Virginia colors knitted into a beautiful new gift, the biggest table doily to date.

The house my girlfriend owns in South Dakota, the house where I park my car with out-of-state plates on the street and sometimes in the driveway, the house decorated with tasteful antiques she bargains for and brings home while I'm away somewhere making photographs, has become, I am glad to say, increasingly decorated by Virginia. For the past year we have called these gifts Virginia, not nap blanket, table doily, scarf, or hat. Virginia is well placed here. Along the top of the sofa in the TV room. Sometimes on the favored table by the front door. And the purple and blue hat now sits atop the plaster bust of a young woman in the guest room. But this house, like my girlfriend, is decidedly private. Now and then I wish we'd throw a big party and share these unusual colors and patterns. But would the neighbors who barely wave care where these gifts come from?

Standing by her rosewood dining room table and matching chairs, my girlfriend pauses and looks at me. She is holding the large, boldly colored table doily that clashes wildly with this interior. It is nearly Christmas.

Where should we put Virginia?

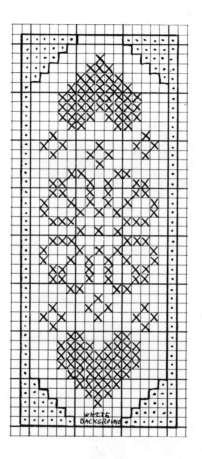

WHITE
BACKGROUND

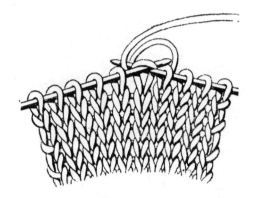

CHESTNUTS

by Betty Christiansen

I found the first ones at my parents' house this summer. I was home for Family Camp, a kind of reunion of the community I grew up in that supplies us with our annual fill of your typical camp activities: singing, crafts, skits, and catching up with old friends. I was digging through the drawers of the dresser in my old room, looking for skit props, when I unearthed two old friends of a different sort: the first two sweaters I had ever made, one knitted, one crocheted. I have a distinct memory of making the knitted sweater: I was sixteen and knitting 4-H projects furiously for the Polk County Fair, near our home in western Wisconsin. That was the year our house had burned down, a chimney fire that had left us homeless in sub-zero January, so I knitted it while sitting cross-legged on the living-room floor of the farmhouse we were renting.

The sweater featured rows of hearts and pine trees and fancy bands in Fair Isle (why start simple?), and skeins of Aunt Lydia's Rug Yarn—a coarse, bulky acrylic yarn that somehow was being marketed as wearable—were tangled everywhere (I had not yet learned how to strand). Miraculously, the pattern was not suffering for the mess; I remember my uncle Arvid and my younger cousin Sarah stopping by, Arvid spying me and telling Sarah, "Look what she can do. Now, you should learn something like that."

The sweater was too big for me, and the sleeves were too big for the armholes, so I made huge tucks in their caps, creating shoulders that stood up and saluted. But it was 1985, and had it fit, I could have been fashionable. I won a grand-champion ribbon on it at the fair (my competition was pot holders and Kleenex-box covers).

I got a blue ribbon on the crocheted sweater, a fuzzy slate blue acrylic, but my memory of making it is murkier. I remember that those sleeves didn't fit either (these I gathered), and that I trimmed its yoke with tiny pink ribbon bows. I repeat, it was 1985.

Skit props these sweaters were not, but they were a fabulous find nonetheless, these twenty-year-old sweaters that I had carefully stitched, put countless hours into, then never wore. I packed them in a grocery bag and brought them to the knitting group that gathered during the afternoon craft period at camp. "Look what I found at Mom and Dad's," I said, and the knitters looked up with glee, then squealed as I pulled each out of the bag.

"They're fantastic!" someone said, and they were: fantastic workmanship, fantastic problem solving, but mostly, fantastically dated.

"I remember wearing sleeves like that," one woman sighed.

"This was a lot of work," a younger knitter said, still unable to quench a snicker. "Look at all those little bows."

"I don't know what to do with them," I admitted. "I'll never use them, but I can't let them go." We all clicked our tongues and shook our heads, for these sweaters were but a token of the myriad abandoned projects—even finished ones—that haunt every knitter's closet. The consensus was that they had to be kept.

"This is a good idea for next year," said Audrey, our knitting craft leader. "Feel free to bring out your old chestnuts, and we can marvel over them all."

I brought the sweaters back to my old bedroom and nestled them back in their drawer lovingly but a little wistfully. It seemed I should take them home with me—but Lord knows I've got plenty of others there.

MY HUSBAND AND I ARE MOVING into a new house this fall, always a good opportunity to sort things out, throw things away. It was easy for me to be ruthless with the Goodwill bag when it came to my husband's drawer of abandoned clothes and the pants I can finally admit I'll never fit into again. The real challenge came when I had to face the winter clothes in storage. For that is where the real population of chestnuts lives—things I knit beautifully, wore once or twice or never, and packed away. I face them every season, every move, and still they cling to me, like silent, neglected children.

These sweaters keep me humble. Reviewing them, I cannot help but wonder why, when I had conquered Fair Isle and intarsia and cables, it took me so long to understand gauge and how to make a sweater that didn't drown me. The worst thing is, I have sweaters I've completed recently that are already doomed for the far corner of winter storage. I'm still making gross miscalculations—sweaters too big, sweaters too short, sweaters with one shoulder in a slightly different yarn because I gambled on the quantity, then ran out. They are too beautiful to tear apart, and I'm too sentimental to give them away. They are chestnuts in waiting, which I'll pull out to show off in twenty more years.

Part of the reason I can't let them go is that, together, they form a sort of knitted history of my life—at least those years I knit sweaters. There are the aforementioned high school sweaters, which never left my parents' home. The college-years sweaters are the ones made in clever, if not bizarre, yarn combinations because all I could afford was the yarn in the bargain bin at Depth of Field in Minneapolis. They reflect the trends of those years, too: the baby pastels and vivid jewel tones of the late eighties; the boxy, shapeless silhouettes; the tight ribbing that made for billowy sleeves. Some illustrate my technical development as a knitter. Take, for instance, the polished-cotton coral tee that was my first foray into lace knitting (never worn, too revealing). Others are travel souvenirs, like the double-breasted cardigan I knit in vivid teal wool from a pattern I picked up on a study-abroad trip to London. Note the striped sleeves: someone ran out of yarn.

There are fewer sweaters in the post-college category, for two reasons: between my copyediting job and a clingy boyfriend, I didn't have much knitting time, and the things I did knit tended, by that point, to be keepers. They fit better, were more classic designs.

Which brings me to a new category of sweaters I can't abandon. These are beloved pieces that were well worn—like the seashell sweater, which I still manage to wear once or twice a year when I know I won't be going out in public. I knit it of heavy cotton yarn I found in a sale bin in some craft store box back in 1990. It was mint green then (it's faded to a dirty off white now) and made from one of the first yarns I knit with that was actually what the pattern had called for. It had that oversized, boxy shape, and I wore it almost exclusively over a slim pair of cropped jeans, with penny loafers and matching mint socks. A large seashell spanned the chest, and I remember how satisfying it was to follow the chart of knit and purl symbols and watch it magically emerge.

I have a distinct memory of knitting this sweater, too. This time, I'm curled up on the leather sofa at my boyfriend's grandparents' house, where he lived while we were in college. The seashell is taking form, and I'm settling into that nirvana that accompanies the execution of a knitting technique that's actually working. His grandmother, Fran, a thoroughly lovable woman who'd had the misfortune of marrying an alcoholic, steps over to peer at the sweater through her bifocals. I can see her artificially champagne-colored curls, her too-bright lipstick on withering lips. She smiles and nods; she's tickled to have a crafty future granddaughter-in-law. I adored Fran and she loved me, but her grandson and I didn't work out. She died before she could learn I had left him, and I was somehow a little grateful for that.

This sweater carries too much for me ever to let it go. In it are memories not only of Fran—her tidy, comfortable house, how she feigned cheerfulness even when her husband berated her—but also the memory of how incredibly good I felt while wearing the sweater. I saved it for exam days when I needed a boost; I wore it on Fridays and my birthday, when I felt like celebrating. Though I can't remember, I like to think it's what I changed into when I came home from a long day at work, or what I reached for every Saturday when the weather turned cool.

I'm sure one of the last times I wore it was when my sister looked at me and said, "That sweater is screaming 'the eighties.'" Or maybe it was the day I picked it up and noticed a distinct yellow edge around the neck and coffee stains smattered across the seashell. I have to admit that another reason I can't give it away is because no one, no matter how needy, would wear it in its present condition. So, for now, I wash it and pack it away in a box marked "Chestnuts."

For with this move, I've decided to quit fooling myself and these poor sweaters, all of whom I do believe have souls, have feelings, and are patiently and hopefully waiting for the day my mind changes, or fashion changes, and they can come back out and be worn as they were first intended to be. I'm not going to shuffle them in and out of storage anymore, but cherish them as the relics they are and let them represent the history they do. For though they are unwearable, I love them all, like children. Like children, they are a part of me.

Maybe I'll do what Audrey suggested and bring them someday to my knitting group, where I'll show them off proudly, if not a little ironically. I won't feel guilty about them, in they way I no longer feel guilty about pages I write and then systematically delete when I realize they're not integral to the story, but were necessary to get it where it needed to be. These sweaters got my knitting—and me—to the place we're at now, and for that, I'm decidedly grateful.

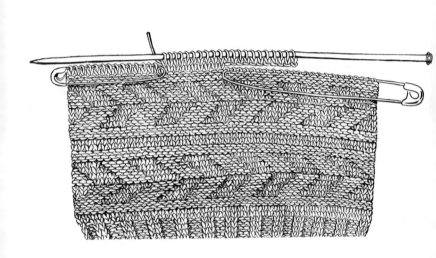

THE AGONY AND THE ECSTASY

by Clara Parkes

To live with knitting is to achieve a state of bliss, an unshakable calm paired with a profound sense of creative fulfillment. The technical term for this is "yarnirvana," and it can take many years to achieve. To get there, most knitters first struggle with sustained periods of restlessness, twitchy fingers, and a need for covert yarn contact at all hours of the day.

The clinical term for this internal disturbance is "yarnilepsy," and it affects as many as one out of every three women in America. Early detection is difficult because it often skips a generation. And in its most infectious state, it can pass from friend to friend—and even stranger to stranger—from nothing more than an innocent, "What are you doing?"

Common symptoms of yarnilepsy include dizziness, sleeplessness, restlessness, a feeling of being overwhelmed, lack of concentration, and an inability to exercise any restraint in yarn-related retail environments. At its worst, yarnilepsy can cause total fiber-induced blackouts. Those who experience this severe state often report an increased quantity of yarn and fiber around them when they regain consciousness—usually in shopping bags accompanied by receipts with staggering totals.

The journey from yarnilepsy to yarnirvana takes time and effort, and unfortunately many knitters give up along the way. If you think you may be contracting yarnilepsy, don't be afraid and don't give up. You can achieve yarnirvana, and its rewards are infinite.

After struggling with yarnilepsy for more than seventeen years and almost giving up completely, I passed to the other side. Let me share my story in the hopes that it'll help make your own journey easier.

As best I can tell, I contracted yarnilepsy from my grandmother during a brief Christmas visit when I was twelve years old. I caught a glimpse of her knitting basket by the fireplace. In it was a mound of butter-colored wool and an unfinished Aran sweater on the needles, bobbles and cables beckoning me. I felt a deep tingling in my fingers, a quickening of the pulse, a magnetic pull between that basket and my body. My mouth opened and out came the words, "Will you teach me to knit?"

We piled into her 1964 Volkswagen Bug and headed to the local yarn shop, located in a cozy old New England farmhouse. We pulled open the squeaky front door and stomped our snowy boots on a sheep-shaped welcome mat. And then I remember catching my first whiff of that spicy, warm, lanolin-infused scent of pure wool.

Life became a dream. Everything around me started to speed and swirl. My pulse quickened. Blood pounded in my ears. My eyes and mouth were frozen open. The throttle on each of my senses was stuck in the full open position, with nothing to filter or slow the inward rush of experience.

Hands reached out to grab skein after skein. I buried my face into them and took deep breaths, as if in an opium-induced state of ecstasy. I wanted all of it—the colors, the textures, the smells. I wanted to possess that yarn, body and soul. My fingers yearned to wrap it swiftly and effortlessly around the needles, like I'd seen my grandmother do so many times. I longed to feel a sublime knitted fabric grow from my very own hands.

I have no memory of the next two weeks. It was as if I'd been abducted by aliens. When I finally came out of it, I was back at my parents' house in Arizona with only a pair of empty needles, a horribly misshapen scarf, and a pile of unfinished homework to mark my binge.

I knew no other knitters, and—with the exception of that sad little scarf—my house was devoid of yarn. I knew of no yarn stores, no books, no magazines, no knitting groups, no nothing. As winter turned to spring and summer, indoor temperatures rose to ninety degrees and my winter wool ecstasy all but evaporated. But it was just a matter of time. I later learned that once you've experienced one yarnileptic seizure, the chances of another one occurring are more than 99.9 percent. It doesn't matter if one year passes, or ten. The magnitude will be just as great if not greater than the last episode.

I grew up, time passed, the yarn returned, and the episodes grew more frequent. As the lure of the yarn got stronger, my ability to put it down weakened. I spent more and more time with my yarn—time that was earmarked for laundry, paying bills, buying groceries, bathing, feeding myself, sleeping. I was spinning out of control, and something needed to be done. So I tried self-medicating my condition.

I first limited my yarn contact to thirty minutes at a time, even setting a clock by my side so I couldn't cheat. But the very first time I tried this, I discovered three days later that the clock—and all the others in my house—had been continually reset as if no time had passed at all. (I still can't imagine why someone would've broken into my house and pulled such a prank.)

Frustrated and fearing I could never live a normal life, I decided to go cold turkey and eliminate all yarn from my environment. This, I discovered, is the worst thing a yarnileptic can do. It triggers severe YDD, or yarn deficit disorder. Even curtain pulls, shoelaces, dental floss, videocassette tapes, and jumper cables could get me started.

About this time I switched jobs and discovered a yarn store not five miles from my office. Lunches stretched from thirty minutes to an hour to two hours and longer. I tried putting just a little change in my parking meter to force shorter visits, but this only resulted in a pile of tickets and an eventual weekend at traffic school (a great place to catch up on your knitting, by the way).

I could handle the dirty laundry, bare kitchen cupboards, and questionable accounting practices. But it was growing clear that my career path—high-tech journalism—and my yarn path could not peacefully coexist. One had to go.

Avoiding the bigger question, I focused on climate. I was living in the San Francisco Bay Area by then, and the moderate temperatures made my wool-constant condition too uncomfortable. So I relocated to Maine where, from a drafty coastal New England farmhouse, I could continue my career while expanding my yarn time in almost total anonymity.

But things only got worse. I started spinning my own yarn. At home. Under cover of darkness. I figured that if I could control my supply, I'd no longer blank out in yarn stores. What I didn't realize is that fiber festivals—which I frequented for my raw materials—caused another equally contagious and severe disorder: fibrolepsy.

By then the yarnilepsy had spread from my hands to my brain, making concentration on anything other than yarn nearly impossible. Deadlines passed, e-mails went unanswered. My career was in peril, and something had to be done.

I decided to seek professional advice. My doctor, a young medical-school graduate who tried hard to conceal his smirk, quickly seized upon my use of the term "anxiety" and suggested I see a psychiatrist.

I went for one visit. Although the woman seemed competent, she kept referring to yarn as "string." Clearly we had no future.

I returned to the smirking MD, whose patience seemed to be wearing thin. "You say your career is in peril?" he asked, tapping his pencil on my file. "Perhaps career counseling is in order." Off I went to the career counselor, a young woman with a tidy bob haircut, bright hazel eyes, a slim figure, boundless energy, and best of all, no smirk.

I launched into my story like a road-weary salesman giving his spiel, waiting for the shuffling of feet, nervous clearing of throat, and furtive jotting of the words "blatant sociopath" on my file.

But she listened intently, nodding in what seemed like genuine understanding and sympathy. When I finished, she paused before speaking. "Your career isn't in peril," she smiled slowly. "It just needs refocusing."

Pulling out a notepad, she continued, "I'm going to map out a potential mode of treatment. It's pretty dramatic, but it may just work."

She scribbled for a moment, tore the sheet off her pad, folded it, and handed it to me. We shook hands, and she started for the door. I carefully unfolded the precious piece of paper. On it were the words, "You must give up your job and make knitting your life."

What?! I glanced at the figure walking away. She had seemed so smart, so sure of herself, so competent, and yet...quit my job?!

But something clicked in my mind. I began hatching a plan to bring heart and hands together. It involved taking my editorial experience with technology product reviews and applying it instead to yarn.

Nonknitters thought I was insane. And yet with each step I took, I could feel the yarnilepsy abate. My new publication, Knitter's Review, launched and grew. And gradually the frustration and twitchy fingers gave way to fulfillment and the justified presence of yarn all around me, all the time. The struggle with yarnilepsy gave way to a daily indulgence in fiber bliss.

I started meeting other people who, given the same advice, left behind successful careers to focus on knitting fulltime. Writers, yarn store owners, pattern designers, spinners, dyers, publishers, breeders, toolmakers, they all had one thing in common: they had battled yarnilepsy and achieved yarnirvana.

Yarnilepsy is a deeply personal state. For me, it's entering a pasture and hearing the bleating of happy sheep. For others, it's the magical moment they pull a skein from the indigo dyepot and its color shifts to an oxygen-provoked blue. Yet others experience it when they receive the first hand-knit incarnation of their designs from a test knitter, or when they see the glimmer of comprehension in a student's eye when she finally understands the knit stitch.

For me, it's the routine realization that my work no longer takes me away from yarn—it is yarn. It's the sight of heaping piles of colorful test swatches and even larger piles of yarn waiting for their turn on the needles. It's the sight of books to be read and tools to try. And always, it's the unspoken kinship and camaraderie I feel when meeting others on the same path.

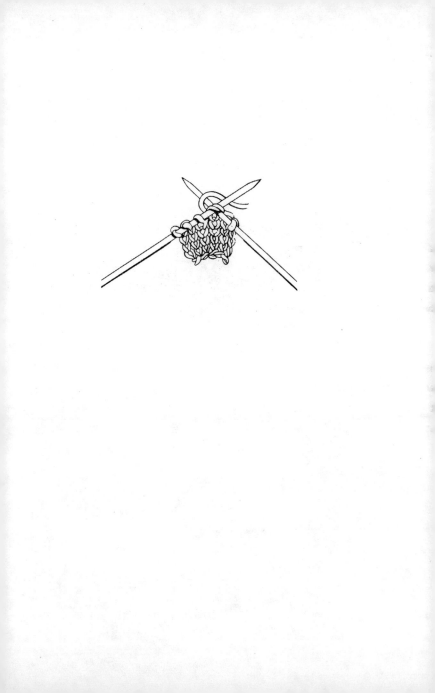

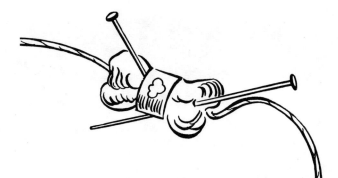

A Knitter's Diary

by Diane Mennella

APRIL 28

Those of us who love our knitting—love the way the needles feel in our hands; love the fiber magically forming into fabric; love the exercise of mind faculties in deciphering the printed symbols of a pattern; love the compliments from friends, family, and especially strangers—find it hard to understand why everyone is not participating in the renaissance of knitting that is made so apparent by the super abundance of local shops and online resources.

Don't even start to tell me what a horrible length of time you spent waiting in the doctor's office/bank-teller line/airport lounge/bus-car-train station because I have no sympathy unless you had your knitting with you to pass the time "constructively," my mother would have said. It's fulfillingly pleasurable, I would add. This raises an interesting point. My mother was a Depression-era bride and being part Scot, to boot, was very careful with the family budget and her time. I've picked up a few of her traits, preferring to daydream only while ironing or folding clothes or knitting a portion of a garment that needs little attention. And I always have either a book or some knitting in a ready-to-go bag "just in case." In fact, when packing for travel of any sort, the more difficult decision is not which shoes but which knitting project to bring.

JUNE 2

Unlike my mother and other necessarily thrifty types, I don't have to knit socks, mittens, sweaters, hats, scarves, dish towels, pot holders, or lace shawls. I have the privilege and freedom to decide that I want to spend the time, money, and energy doing so. Some critics, with whom I have lived, would prefer that not so much time, money, and energy went into the pursuit of my knitting. And I'll admit, perhaps a bit of time budgeting to allow for some floor sweeping would be a good thing. I still like to do the laundry, even though as a city girl, it means getting it to and from a laundromat. But you can guess what's in the shopping cart along with the dirty clothes, detergent, and quarters for the machine.

I can't possibly show up without something new on my needles to share with Nancy, the laundry proprietress. Nancy is one of my biggest knitting fans. She is Chinese-American and communicates with her Mexican-American and Bangladeshi-American employees in an utterly fascinating but completely incomprehensible (to me) patois, which somehow makes perfect sense to all three of them, who all can, additionally, easily communicate with their largely English-speaking clientele. Nancy knits and crochets for her grandchildren without the use of written patterns. One reason she is always so eager to see what I'm up to is that she learns new stitches by watching someone else knit them. Shaping of garments is all by trial and error for her. No gauge swatching, no mailing off to Wisconsin for the exact yarn called for in the latest magazine. She uses what materials she finds and depends on her own ideas for the texture and shape of a particular project. She has a lot in common with the Eastern European ladies who used to populate Manhattan's Lower East Side yarn shops, except they would, if pressed, write out a pattern for you. Kind of like some computer programs—plug in the desired sleeve length, neck style, and stitch pattern, along with your gauge, and, voilá, a pattern to follow at home. I really admire people like Nancy, not relying on a piece of paper to get started.

JUNE 14

Another story from the laundry. Nancy has a daughter, and the daughter's in-laws are immigrants from China and speak very little English. They have been helping out at the laundromat, mostly because they want to be doing something.

The daughter's mother-in-law has noticed my knitting. Yesterday, when the temperature outside was around 100 degrees and I was the only one foolish enough to appear at the laundromat as a self-help customer, she gestured that she would like to hold my knitting. I was struck with the graceful, comfortable way she held my needles; this made it clear to me that she was a knitter, too. She examined the piece (it was a bookmark on eleven stitches worked in crochet thread—a great hot-weather activity) and immediately purled the row, very sweetly asking for confirmation at each stitch to determine that the pattern required a purl. I was thrilled by the wordless connection we made.

AUGUST 25

Have just come back from a charming bookstore devoted entirely to cookbooks and related food matters, where I attended a reading from a recently published book about food, recipes, memories, experiences good and bad concerning meals, followed by a good deal of discussion about restaurants here and abroad. I always feel quite lost in such gatherings. Not that I don't like to eat, but it never was that important to me. At any rate, I was clever enough to marry a fellow who adores working in the kitchen, has a lovely sense of taste combinations, and can make a meal from anything at hand. This does mean that it is my husband who has the fascinating food conversations with my women friends, his in-laws (my sisters), and his children. In fact, when our children left the nest, they would call, say hello to me when I answered the phone, and invariably ask to speak to their dad because they needed suggestions about what to fix for dinner. Only once or twice have they asked for suggestions regarding knitting.

In fact, it is my son-in-law who is the most enthusiastic knitter among all my "extended" children. I taught him the basics one New Year's Eve because his wife, my daughter, went out to do a midnight run in Central Park and left us to babysit. What could be more natural than having your mother-in-law teach you how to knit at midnight? He had confessed to me earlier that his mother had taught him to crochet, but that he had only ever got to make chains, yards and yards of crochet chains. He noticed that I was working with a circular needle, and he asked if I thought he could learn how to knit. "Of course," sez I, and he did. Great fun. Everyone in the family had hand-crafted hats, each of a different design, made by my son-in-law, the following Christmas.

NOVEMBER 19

I always have more than one project "in the bags." I never hesitate to figure out a new technique or play with a new fiber even though I may have several items on the needles needing attention. I've never been disciplined enough to finish one before starting another, even though my mother tried to teach me this lesson, too. When I was about ten years old, I wanted to enter a contest sponsored by a girl's magazine that entailed designing and making a doll. I decided to make mine special, with a wig made from hair that had been cut from my own head. Well, many frustrating and tearful hours later, I threw a proper, frightening tantrum and refused to have anything more to do with the doll. "Oh no," said my mother. "You will finish it the best way you can." And I suppose I did, but truly my heart was not in it.

For sure, this episode did not make the point that one should finish what one starts.

One sweater that I did finish knitting when I was in high school was a beautiful cable-patterned jacket worked with doubled threads of worsted weight yarn. My mother offered to pay—I can't remember if this was a reward for completing the sweater or an incentive— to have it finished professionally: blocked and assembled, including the separating zipper in the front opening. I foolishly left it behind in a ladies room in college. Never did recover it or see it on campus anywhere.

A few years later, I began to work on an afghan made of sampler-type squares. This one was assembled by me and was used and abused by my young family. I seem to recall that it "grew" several holes, principally along the seam lines, and somehow found its way into the laundry dryer, where a bit of felting occurred. As I think about these two instances, I'm not surprised that I'm singularly unregretful about them. Because for me, the process of knitting is what satisfies me, not necessarily reveling in the finished product.

DECEMBER 17

The theme of a short essay I wrote a few years ago expressed how connected I feel to all who have associated themselves through history with the craft of knitting. By the very actions of thinking about a project; choosing a yarn, a pattern, a technique; casting on, working, finishing, I feel I'm in the same room, as it were, with everyone who has ever done the same. They may be third-century Egyptian, twelfth-century Flemish, twenty-first-century Tlingit. What a wide circle of friends!

JANUARY 19

Posted on the bulletin board of a community garden in my neighborhood today was a poem by one of the English romantics, extolling the necessity of gardens. I stopped to read it, but was more struck with the fact that it had been typed on an old Smith-Corona or similar manual typewriter—noticeable because of the typeface, which no computer font has yet duplicated. I marveled that the machine still worked (I discarded mine about twenty years ago). And this led to my thinking of the ease with which we discard the out-of-date and latch onto the new. When it comes to knitting, I think how wonderful it is to keep alive something that connects us through the ages without growing old and useless. I've had people ask me, "Why are you knitting socks when you can get perfectly good ones for not much money?" I usually smile to myself and think about how it costs no money at all to keep alive a skill like knitting and pass it along, simply by doing it. And how much more important that is than just covering someone's feet.

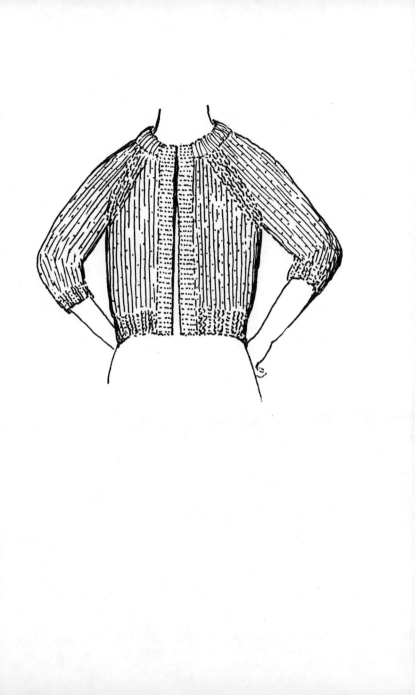

LEARNING TO LIVE IN THE SLOW PROCESS

by Eiko Berkowitz

TWENTY YEARS IN NEW YORK CITY

I t has been almost twenty years since I arrived in New York City from Tokyo. I had so many hopes when I came here and saw the seemingly limitless possibilities of life in this new land. While Japan has a very deep culture, it is rather narrow in its scope. America, on the other hand, is not deep in its culture because it has only existed for a very short time, but its range of options is very wide. This is the land of personal freedom. Japan is lagging behind in women's freedom, for example, and the business world is run primarily by men. This makes it much harder for a woman to be creatively free.

After I arrived, I began exploring New York City from morning to night. I did not want to miss anything. I found many new things here, although there were certain things I had to give up. My master's degree in social work was not recognized, so I could not continue in my work with homeless people and children with disabilities. I was also lonely, so far away from my family and friends. I missed the exceptional food available in Tokyo, and I missed going to the mountains to sit in the therapeutic hot springs, where wild monkeys actually come into the bath with you. I did find the Russian baths in the East Village, though. I made many new friends, who I continue to visit even now. I found lots of different ethnic foods that are not generally available in Japan. And I continue to take care of street cats.

I set my sights on getting a green card so I could legally live in the United States and work to earn a living. You have to have a sponsor and a good reason why you should be allowed to stay. Additionally, the government wants to know that you are not taking a job away from a U.S. citizen. I found a job in a great Japanese restaurant called Meriken in the Chelsea section. My official title was "banquet decorator." This basically required skills that only a person trained in the fine art of Japanese culture and cuisine would have, such as sado (tea ceremony), ikebana (flower arrangement), syuji (calligraphy), and kaiseki ryori (Edo period cooking).

Eventually, I reached my second goal of opening my own restaurant, in 1991. It was called Pacific Rim, and the menu included dishes that married tastes and textures from all sides of the Pacific Ocean, from South America, through California and Alaska, over to Japan, Korea, China, Vietnam, Thailand, Indonesia, and even Australia.

TREASURE BOX

I worked very hard to achieve my goals, but to do so I had to focus all of my energy. I forgot about knitting during these first years in New York. About four or five years ago, I got out of the restaurant business, and I began to settle down and live a calmer life. I found that I no longer had a constant need for excitement. Finally, I had time to go through my personal treasure box, which contained many beautiful things from my life in Japan. I had stashed away all the important things, so many experiences and my many other abilities, while I was working so hard in the restaurants and to get my green card. I had a small collection of beautiful clothing from my mother, grandmother, and great-grandmother (I grew up in a house with four generations). I also had some fabrics, yarn, knitting needles, and even some small ceramic pieces. I had two sweaters that I had made in Japan more than twenty-five years earlier. These were literally my family treasures. But my box also, figuratively, included all of my creative talents. I remember putting these things away and telling them, "I'll see you later."

On one excursion to the East Village, I discovered a small yarn shop called Downtown Yarns. This was the first time I'd found a collection of beautiful yarn like what I could buy in Japan when I was young. This event really triggered my reawakening. It was as if Rita, the owner, had rubbed my personal Aladdin's lamp and out came my forgotten talent as a knitter.

(RE)LEARNING KNITTING

Hanging around Rita rekindled my love for making things. There was something about her that just clicked with my personality. She made my insides scream, "I want to make something. I want yarn!" I was so impressed with Rita's character that I went to Downtown Yarns every day and met more beautiful people. I then met a woman who became my teacher.

She has no rules about how to knit. Actually, she is very particular and knows a lot of rules. But she also understands that the value of discipline is to know when to go outside yourself. Discipline is what gives you the ability to directly connect your heart to your hands without your head getting in the way. This is why you have to play your scales before you can be a great piano player, for example; eventually your fingers just go to the right places without thinking about it. My teacher is wacky and good crazy in this way. She also teaches that a mistake is not a bad thing. It may be the path to creating something new and different and wonderful.

In the beginning, I always had to have a dictionary with me, because while I knew how to speak English, I did not know the English knitting vocabulary. Finally, my teacher taught me enough and gave me the confidence to be able knit without a dictionary. It was like "knitting without tears." That was an important step for me.

INDIVIDUAL STYLES AND NEEDS: MAKING MY OWN YARN

I found that the rules were too limiting and boring; when I tried to follow them, I discovered that I was doing my own thing. Then I realized that I had developed my own set of rules—things that do not necessarily work for anyone else. But I continued to take classes because my teacher taught me more options, and that gave me more courage. One day she told me that the most fun part of knitting is choosing colors. I think I have an instinctual color sense. As soon as I see one color, I can visualize what else goes with it. But I also like the textures, yarn next to yarn, yarn next to my skin. The texture is closely related to the color. I am drawn to irregular surfaces, perhaps because I grew up with a small barnyard of animals: cows, goats, chickens, rabbits, cats, and a dog, at my Tokyo house.

I wanted to learn more, so Rita gave me the phone number for the two women, mother and daughter, who teach at the Spinner's Hill Workshop near Bainbridge in upstate New York, tucked between the Catskill and Adirondack mountains. The farm has 350 acres with a lake, a Victorian house, a workshop studio, and a barn with a silo. They have more than 200 sheep, and goats, pigs, turkeys, geese, dogs, and cats.

They have been teaching me to shear the sheep, wash and dry the wool, dye the wool, wash and dry again, spin the wool into yarn, and then knit. This is a really slow process. The preparation is very important; I appreciate this, and I love this way of working. It reminds me of my old days in the kitchen in Japan, working with my family.

When I go up there, I usually stay for a week. We meet in the house and have breakfast together. Lisa tells me what to work on that day and I go off to the workshop. She checks in on me and later we have lunch and discuss my progress. I work again until dinnertime, when we all eat together again. Lisa's mom is a great cook and I bring up Japanese foods for them to try as well. It is a funny mix of cultures.

The progression from dying to spinning is a most interesting process. We shear the sheep and wash and dry the raw locks of wool. Then I can dye the raw wool any color I like. I lean toward bright Kool-Aid colors, but like subtle ones as well, depending on what I will be making. There are variations in the wool itself that makes it take differently. To make even more interesting color combinations, we card the wool and mix the colors. Carding is sort of like running a big comb through the locks to make it into long, fine strands of fiber. The wool maintains its irregularities in texture even after all of this processing. Each batch is one of a kind. It is more beautiful and natural than commercially produced wool.

I spun with a drop spindle for a couple of years. I really like this way of working because I can do it anywhere. I can even drop-spin on the New York City subway. Everyone looks at me to figure out what the heck I am doing. It is a very addictive process. I spin until I drop (pun intended). Then one evening Lisa forced me to try the spinning wheel. I resisted at first, but the wheel eventually changed my life. You have to be coordinated to use the wheel, but it becomes like meditation. I spin outside and the animals all come to keep me company.

Felting is another process that we do at the workshop. It is laborious, because you have to rub the wool fibers by hand until they become matted. It takes long time and you have to be careful to keep the wool even. It is another example of a slow process that I really enjoy—one that produces something with a lot of heart.

A side benefit to being up on the sheep farm is that baby lambs are often being born. I enjoy feeding the new babies from a bottle whenever the mother doesn't take care of them. I have spent my whole life taking care of animals. I used to rescue cats from the streets of Tokyo and now do the same here in New York. I have nine cats at the moment, six at home and three more in my store. They bring me great joy. And they really love to play with the raw wool.

All my work with yarn is a slow process. When I live in Manhattan, everything is so fast. Now I really enjoy this slow life. I enjoy the processing and also the preparation. This is the way I am going to live the rest of my life—slowly, with careful consideration of all the details.

BROKEN FOOT: MAKING SOCKS

I was getting ready to go up to the mountains to attend the April class when I fell off a five-foot-high ladder and broke my heel. I learned that it would take almost six months to recover. Fortunately, I still had my two hands, so I could work on my knitting. I could not put any weight on my foot, so I gathered up all of my knitting tools and materials and then stayed in my bed and worked. Everything was an arm's length away.

One day I really had pain, so my husband helped me by pulling out a big box full of yarn, and by chance, I found wool for socks. It was sort of ironic, however, that I would be knitting socks with a broken foot. This was really an opportunity. I was so isolated because I could not even go out of my house. So I took advantage of making socks to relieve my frustration. Knitting the socks reminded me of my experiences as a child.

CHILDHOOD KNITTING

When I was little, we all used to work in the kitchen together. I would be sitting in the kitchen, watching, helping with the cooking. We lived four generations in one house, fourteen people all together: two sets of great-grandparents, two sets of grandparents, my parents, and my brothers and sister and me. We were all living together in a traditional-style Japanese house made of wood and paper. It was like what you see in a samurai movie, with sliding shoji screen doors, tatami mats on the floor, and very minimal furniture. There is a cooking style called irori, where a pot is hanging from the ceiling over a fire made from charcoal and everything cooks very slowly. The meals cooked like this usually contain dried beans and roots and other vegetables, which make a nice stew, like a hot pot. No one leaves while the food is cooking because the pot has to be watched. This is another example of slow processing.

So everyone sat around the cooking space and talked about their own topics, and they would knit. I would sit watching them and they started to teach me how to knit. That was my first experience with knitting. I was four years old.

Now I am sitting in my bed thinking about all these things while I am knitting socks. This broken foot gave me the opportunity to slow down so much. It gave me the ability to remember all my past experiences. I also remembered that when I was in the fourth grade I took a class in which the girls had to knit a pair of socks. That was my first pair of socks. They were blue. They had a lot of holes, so they were sort of a disaster, but it is a great memory anyway. I am sure my mother still has them somewhere.

I remember one day, when all four generations were sitting around, I came to a realization. I looked down at the vest I was wearing and asked my mother, "Is this my father's sweater?" "Yes, and now it is your vest," she replied. They took apart my father's clothing and remade that material into a tiny vest for me to wear. Nothing is ever wasted in Japan because we have so few resources. That was my first experience with recycling materials and remaking clothing. This philosophy carries on today in my store, where I sell Japanese designer clothing secondhand.

PERSONAL VISION

My small clothing store on the Lower East Side of Manhattan features the work of individual designers. These are people who create unique pieces with a "different" eye that is somewhat aligned with my vision. I am interested in three particular elements of design: asymmetrical shape, color, and layering.

My sense of shape may originate with Rei Kawakubo, the creator of Comme des Garçons, a Japanese clothing design company. She was the first person in fashion to really break rules, like not having the shoulder end where a person's shoulder really ends, and everything is very off center, and geometric but asymmetrical. It is more like wearing a sculpture than just clothing. These designs were all black in the late 1970s, inspired by the many ravens in Tokyo.

My sense of color was greatly influenced by my dear friend Amy Downs, who designs hats that range from very formal to totally outrageous. Actually, even the formal designs are outrageous. She will use any raw material that strikes her eye. She did a series of hats decorated with the plastic bags they use in Chinatown. The bags are all different colors, and when mixed together almost look like a bouquet of flowers the way they are cut and folded. I would go down to her store and hang out with her every Sunday beginning in the mid 1980s. I would come home every week with six or eight new hats. I now own more than 800 hats by Amy. Her bright colors influenced me; I started to dress my body to look like her hats. I was in full bloom.

Then I started to layer clothing so that just a small piece of something would be sticking out from underneath. I like how layered clothing changes as you move. One friend named Heide Yip works in a similar way. She travels all over the world collecting material. Some is vintage, some is new, but it is all very beautiful and unique. Then she combines these together to make one-of-a-kind-pieces by hand. These take a long time to make. They are exactly to my taste.

SLOW PROCESSING: PHILOSOPHY

Making soap has the same slow preparation and processing time as working with yarn. I produce my own line of handmade soaps that include Japanese mayu (golden silk), which has a healing capability for the skin. It takes a couple of days to "cook up" all the ingredients. Even after the soap is taken out of the molds and cut into bars, it takes three to four weeks for it to cure. I enjoy being surrounded by many small bars of soap drying on racks all around my apartment as I pursue my knitting. I am still making them even though I am not touching them. It is a slow, passive involvement, but this allows me to be creating in two different ways at the same time—knitting and soap making. The smell of the soap and the feel of the yarn—everything becomes part of the same complimentary environment.

This slow processing reminds me of the days of my childhood. The slow cooking and the knitting and the soap making all run together. And this philosophy of slowness extends to all things in my life. It is also a way to build my personal community. I now work with friends who are artists and designers—makers of beautiful things. This life with my new friends is just like my life with my family when I was little. And the knitting is figuratively and literally what ties us together.

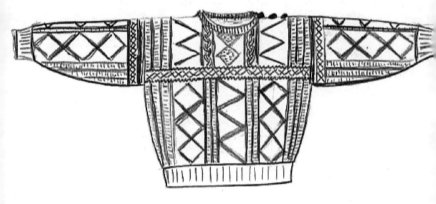

Illustration by Caroline Herzog

LITTLE GUERNSEY

by Caroline Herzog

"Oh, what a cute sweater; did you knit that?"

To have community is wonderful, wherever one is. But in a rural area like the one I live in, in Ripton, Vermont, community can almost be magical. After our first child, Thomas, was born, my husband, Michael, and I were surprised by our community with one of the most amazing gifts we have ever received: six weeks of meals delivered to our house on every Tuesday and Thursday. Such meal deliveries are usually organized by friends or by a person in town, who decides that something should be done to welcome and to help out. There is no real order or hierarchy to who makes the first call to ask you if you would like to become a part of the meal calendar, which is intended not only to welcome babies, but also to help a family when illness or other hardships strike. The meals are usually composed of a salad, a main dish such as a soup or a casserole, bread, dessert, and something to drink—enough for the whole family for one meal, sometimes two. They arrive at dinnertime. In our case, it was not just food that was brought, but also hand-me-downs, like a child's favorite cup, books, a soft and fuzzy hat with silly-looking bear ears that had already seen much love; something small and personal that would continue the web of community and goodwill down the line.

With the birth of our second child, Phoebe, the same most generous meal calendar was reintroduced. As the first blustery, cold January days of Phoebe's life went by, friends dropped in to bring good food and good company, and to meet the newest addition to town. And once again, some also came with meaningful tokens from their own past or from their children's pasts. One late afternoon, my dear friend and neighbor Linda came by with Thomas's favorite meal, pizza. She turned on our oven and started to unpack. Out of her basket came the fresh pizza, already on the paddle; a pot of hearty root-vegetable soup for Michael and me; flowers; desert; and a salad.

"Wow," I thought. "I never eat quite this well." Here was plenty of food to last us for at least two days, both lunches and dinners. Then Linda said with a smile: "We have a little something for Phoebe." Linda lifted a package of brightly colored tissue paper adorned with a white, silky ribbon from the basket and handed it to me.

"It's not much," she said, "only an old but favorite hand-me-down that both my kids wore." I unfolded the tissue to reveal the soft treasure it was harboring. Inside, I discovered the sweetest little pale yellow wool sweater, a guernsey, with a thin orange- and lime-colored Fair Isle diamond band across the chest. I was stunned to receive such a gift; items such as these normally stay within a family and are eventually packed up in a box and placed in an attic, only to be rediscovered years later, smelling of stale, dusty heat and pungent mothballs. Now here was this treasure in my hand, passed on for us to love.

I HAVE BEEN A HAPPY KNITTER since learning the craft in school in Austria, where I grew up. Knitting hats, mittens, and sweaters has been my passion. My first sweater was a raglan multistripe; I think it was composed of six different colors, with stripes of random widths. The project was a bit of overkill for a novice knitter, but now, in retrospect, I see that it was a good challenge. Throughout my knitting of it, I remember I found myself green with envy for my best friend, Renate, who was knitting a mohair sweater with dropped shoulders on size 10 needles and only one color. We were quite competitive with each other, only it was never an open competition, just an unspoken drive to finish first. She won this particular challenge—my size 6 needles and six colors just could not compete. From then on, I knit Portuguese fisherman look-alike sweaters, changing the yoke and shoulder pattern slightly, or the waistband, to make them just a bit more interesting. I have no idea how many of these I ultimately knit, first for myself and then for friends. The remnants I would knit up into alpine ski hats, playing with two or three color patterns and designs as I went, always improving on the last hat. My stash was quickly used up, given away as presents.

As I matured, my knitting matured as well. One day, sitting in the sun on the front patio of my father's house in Austria, my stepmother and I had one of our best conversations. It was about knitting. When my two-week stay was over, she gave me a book that had just been published by the name of Bäuerliches Stricken 2 by Lisl Fanderl. It was a collection of stitch and cable patterns from the different provinces and valleys of Austria, each having its own character and meaning, such as a pattern found only among the people of the Inntal region, or a pattern meaning "open love" that would be given to someone when their love was accepted and out in the open. It is a fabulous book, with a wealth of information, and one that has broadened and challenged my knitting over the years. After receiving it, I started to design my own cable sweaters, playing around with what the book had to offer and knowing I had 220 stitches for which to find patterns.

The sweater I loved most I knit from wool a family friend spun from her sheep. The wool was the color of crushed blueberries, absolutely beautiful. I gave the sweater to my sister, who kept it stashed in her closet. I recently stole it back from her.

The process of knitting is what keeps bringing me back to it—the act of creating, of watching patterns unfold and shapes evolve and fall down from the needles methodically, row by row, from only a thread that before held nothing and kept nothing warm. Most times, I let the yarn inspire my next project, sitting with a skein of it in hand as I contemplate what to knit next. Or I'll see a cable that fascinates me and I'll have to use it somehow in a sweater. Or I'll see a stitch pattern that's just too cool, like a blossom-twig pattern. How does it work, and why, and best of all, what brilliant person thought it up?

Until recently, I never followed a pattern. Learning to knit in Austria is more about learning to knit with what yarn you have on hand. Our knitting teacher was one of the town's ladies, who would come in to school one afternoon a week and teach all the girls, starting in second grade, how to sew, macramé, embroider, crochet, and knit. She would show up with her large, brown, plastic-rimmed glasses perched on her nose; hand-knit white cotton lace knee socks pulled up to just under her kneecap; pleated loden-colored wool skirt; shoes that had been well worn but were meticulously maintained with lots of shoe polish; a white blouse buttoned all the way up to the collar. A strand of enormous imitation pearls adorned her neck and chest. Her hair was wavy, shoulder length, light brown with gray streaks every now and then, and seemed to be puffy and somewhat unruly—surprisingly out of control. She carried herself properly and spoke with a stiff lip, and would look down her nose through her glasses at us. To a child, she seemed unapproachable, and I had the feeling that if I went to her for help or with a question, I'd better have a good reason.

The boys got to learn the skills of building, carving, and making things simply out of wood. Before we got to the knitting part of our class, I was always wishing I could be doing what the boys where doing. (Times have changed in Austria, too; now, boys learn to knit and sew and girls chisel.) Sewing was absolutely frustrating for me. The Austrians' ever-present need for perfection was difficult for me to uphold, and I was a far cry from a perfect Austrian seamstress. It seemed silly to me to have to baste stitch everything before you could sew it on the sewing machine, and thus I would try to take shortcuts, resulting in my having to sit and tear everything out again and again because the lines were not perfectly straight. By the time I got to sew the fabric for what would be its final joining, the material always looked tired and a bit worn out. Knitting, however, was something I grew to love. It was very much like building, one block—or in this case one stitch—at a time, and I didn't have to worry about taking fabric and cutting it too big or much worse, "Oh je!!@#*!" too small. There was no need to worry; if I made a mistake, I could just unravel it and reknit it as perfect as it needed to be to make my teacher happy.

We learned to knit as most do. Bringing our own needles and wool to class, we learned to cast on, knit, purl, increase and decrease a stitch, and, finally, to cast off. Much to my mother's chagrin, because I used up much of her precious yarn, we made way too many pot holders in order to practice our stitches. Austrians like the act of repetition; it forces perfection and "Ordnung muss sein!" (There must be order!). It can drive some people crazy, as it did my sister a few years earlier, when she was learning to knit the heel and gusset of a sock. After the teacher demanded that she tear out the portion for the fifth time because it was not perfect, my sister stormed to the fourth-story window, opened it, and launched her knitting to the ground. Plop! The sock landed in a heap, and the ball of yarn attached to it rolled silently into the street; only the clinking of metal needles on the asphalt sidewalk was audible. The act was deemed a very serious offense—the needles could have hit someone, after all—and my sister was forced to carry out her penance: knit more heels! She still refuses to knit a sock to this day.

Finally, after mastering our stitches, we were able to move on to knitting a cat, our first true project. Mine turned out to be a pretty funny-looking cat, white and floppy, with a tail that was much too long for any earthly cat. The face was stitched on and had a bit of a Cheshire-cat look about it. Actually, it was a bit scary and ultimately horrid-looking, with haunting yellow and black eyes and a strange, unnatural grin. I'm not sure what became of it; maybe it just didn't make it into the shipping crate when we moved from Austria to the United States.

After the cat project, we would start all projects by casting on twenty-two stitches and knitting a ten-centimeter-gauge swatch with whatever yarn we were using. If we were to knit a hat, we would have to measure our head and figure out how many stitches to cast on to fit our knitting gauge. After knitting a handsome tube, we would be walked through the decrease method and, voilá, a hat was born. Mittens went much in the same manner: increase for the palm, this is how the thumb is knit, and this is how the fingertips are made; write it all down so that you remember to do the same for the second mitten. By seventh grade, we had moved on to sweaters. Here we used brown packing paper, drew the sweater of our choice onto it, and after decoding what our yarn and needle combination would produce for a gauge, we would cast on and start knitting, following the contours of what we had drawn.

ALL THIS CAME BACK TO ME over the next days and weeks as I looked at the little guernsey sweater Linda had brought. The sweater is well made and carefully knit, something any order-loving Austrian would be proud of. It is a simple sweater, with dropped shoulders knit in DK-weight wool. Carrying a lovely guernsey pattern of zigzags and diamonds that begin to unfold after the waistband, across the chest runs that simple, horizontal orange and lime green Fair Isle band, adding a happy and joyful spark to the sweater. Above the Fair Isle band, the pattern switches slightly to one of a central diamond composed of knit and purl stitches; to either side of the diamond, like Greek revival columns, are two true four-stitch cables, strengthening the sweater's presence, like pillars flanking the gate of a garden. The sleeves display the same diamond pattern as the body, with the Fair Isle band capping them at their tops. Across the left shoulder are three small, white ceramic buttons to allow the collar to open further, enabling the head of a child to pass through with ease.

The seams and the collar of the sweater are finished with wonderful precision, alluding to the skill of someone with many years of practice. Feeling the stitches between my fingers, neat and tight, I imagined an older woman knitting for a daughter or son, a neighbor or friend, who was soon to become a parent. I pictured her as a knitter with many years of experience, fingers agile and quick even though arthritis had gnarled the joints of her hands, sitting in the comfort of her home, where she had raised her own family and knit countless other sweaters.

Linda was not sure who had knitted the sweater; she thought maybe it had been Doc Simon's wife, an elderly lady who had been an avid knitter until she had passed away the previous year. Linda had received the sweater as a hand-me-down from a mutual friend, whose two children had worn it as well. One of these children is a spirited, blue-eyed, curly-haired blonde who looked like a little angel as a baby yet had the playfulness of a forest elf. Living as she was, surrounded by national forest, how could she not pass her childhood like an elf, catching the early morning dew dropping off leaves, plunging into the pond after frogs and salamanders, wobbling from stone to stone, all the while wearing the little yellow guernsey that now was in my hands. Her traces on the sweater are those of use. The friend's second child, a strong-willed boy, grew to play in the same woods with his older sister; eventually, he was big enough to be kept warm by the same little guernsey. He found the blueberry bushes to be the best spots for hiding; they were like a maze that only he could navigate. Hands full of blueberries and the occasional cranberry, he would fill his mouth till his belly was happy. And yes, he added plenty of blueberry stains to the sweater.

The guernsey landed in Linda's hands when she had her first child, a boy. His dark brown eyes and dark hair seemed to be a natural complement to the yellow, and especially the orange and lime green of the Fair Isle band. He would leave traces of everyday life on the sweater, as would his younger brother after him. Tumbling and playing hard as children do, eating and spilling juice, wiping sticky hands on anything readily available so as not to have to interrupt what you are doing, will leave marks, showing the passage of time, of lives being lived.

By the time the sweater had been passed on to us, it had lost a bit of its looseness from being washed once (or maybe a couple of times) too vigorously. It looked like it had had a slight but accidental felting, and was thus thicker and fuzzier than it started out. But it was beautiful and sweet nevertheless. Phoebe grew and was able to wear the sweater for its first outing in the spring. Finally, those cold days passed, and one glorious spring day we could go and play outside in the grass. It was still early enough in the year that the famous biting fly of the northeast woods, known here as the black fly, was not out yet, and we were left in peace to enjoy the outdoors. The sun was warm, but there was still a cool spring breeze in the air. Too early to be planting vegetables, but not too early to dream about what would go where. The sight of the dark, warm soil drew me in, and I pulled weeds and filtered the dirt that would soon become our garden through my fingers.

Phoebe joined the weed-tugging game, although she soon found that dirt was much more fun to play in than weeds were to pull. Digging her pudgy little baby hands into the warm and sticky brown soil, she quickly became covered from head to toe in it, and then progressed to eating it as well. Looking over at her, I thought to discourage her meal, all the while hearing my husband's voice in my head, which diminished my urgency: "Well, you gotta eat a peck of dirt before you die." Struggling with whether I should leave her to explore her surroundings or pull her away, I finally decided to let her be. She played happily for a while, then discovered a watering can leaning up against the fence post at the edge of the garden. She stopped what she was doing, ambled over to the can, grabbed it, pulled it over to our future garden, and to her and my surprise, discovered there was water in it. In an instant, Phoebe had transformed her play area into a mud pit. And suddenly, with horror and disgust, I realized that the little guernsey was part of the mud bath.

Phoebe managed to cover herself and the sweater completely in mud in the time it took me to cross the garden. Standing up, she wiped her filthy hands across her chest and stomach. Upset with myself for being so careless, I scooped Phoebe up, whisked her inside and straight to the bath. I placed her, clothing and all, in the tub, where I began to strip her down and rinse her off. I took the sweater and shook it out, and then submerged it in cold water. But the knowledge of how to remove deep, dark, organic mud from a pale yellow wool sweater is not my specialty. Phoebe, of course, thought the whole thing to have been a great adventure and came squeaky clean in an instant. Not so the little guernsey. I washed it four times with two different wool soaps. I let it sit for many hours to soak, hoping to loosen up the stain, but the tannins of the soil were too strong. The cuffs refused to come clean. Rubbing them together, I became as obsessed as Shakespeare's Lady Macbeth; those damned spots did not want to come out! The sweater now had Phoebe written all over it, and we, too, had left our mark.

A year later, I found myself pursuing a life's dream of surrounding myself with wool and color. Driven by a force I'm at a loss to explain, I purchased the remains of a local yarn store, renovated a space in an early 1800s farmhouse my husband and I have owned for the past seventeen years and used to live in, and started my own business. Yes, a yarn shop. The boxes started to arrive in late November and I began filling empty cubbies, now standing in what once had been our living room, with colorful, fuzzy pearls, brimming with the potential of creativity. Needing things with which to decorate the store, I pulled together all the handknitted items I owned, of which one was the little guernsey sweater. Hanging these things on the walls, over the mantle of the fireplace, and behind the woodstove, and stuffing the hats I had knit with tissue paper and placing them on top of the cubbies amongst the books, gave the shop the finishing touches I desired.

The first winter I was open for business, my friend Sheryl came in to check out the new store. We had not seen one another in many months, amazing when we only live six miles from one another. It was fun to welcome her into the new space, since the last time she had seen it was years before, when it had been my living and dining rooms. The day was cold, dark, and blustery, a blue-gray February afternoon. I had lit the woodstove in the morning and placed a pot of water on top, to give the dry air some moisture. By the afternoon, the fire radiated its warmth throughout the shop and provided a cozy place to sit. Sheryl admitted to me that things were not going well in her marriage, and that it would be coming to an end in the near future. She seemed to be feeling quite blue, and like she needed some conversation, so I offered her a cup of tea, and we sat at the back of the shop and chatted.

Suddenly, as if she had seen a ghost from her past, she looked up. Something had caught her eye. Her mouth fell open and she turned to me, pointing to the wall where the little guernsey was hanging. In a stunned and disbelieving voice she said, "Oh my God, I knit that! How did you get it? That's the sweater I knit for Brianna when I was pregnant!" Telling the story of how the sweater had come to us, I felt we had come full circle. Only now I knew it was not an elderly lady who had knit the sweater, but a young woman, a friend, awaiting her firstborn child. This came as an absolute surprise to me. I had never even known that Sheryl could knit.

Sheryl began to sit a little more upright now. She seemed to be feeling a bit better, certainly proud of the fact that her sweater was still around and actually hanging on display. She finished her cup of tea, placed it on the table, and said, "Well, I've got to go pick up the kids from school. Thanks for the tea and for cheering me up a bit." With that, she left the store. Sheryl could not remember what pattern she had used, only that she had borrowed a book from a friend, and that was over twelve years ago. So the pattern remained a mystery to me.

A couple of months passed. People would come in to the store and inevitably comment on the sweater. It just has the power to make people smile and say: "Oh, what a cute sweater; did you knit that?" Or they would ask, "Do you have the pattern for that sweet little sweater?" My response was always the same, and I would hand them a pattern that was close but did not include the Fair Isle band. One day, after receiving another box full of new and classic pattern books for the store, I leafed through the stack of children's books. Suddenly, there it was, the guernsey with the Fair Isle band running through it, in New Baby Knits by Debbie Bliss. At last I had fully unraveled the mysteries of the little sweater. At present, it is still hanging in my store, inspiring people and making them smile. But one day soon it will move on to its next, as of yet undetermined, adventure, to fill someone else's heart with a smile.

Illustration by Lydia Vivante

WOOL, WOAD, WELLFLEET

by Lydia Vivante

My sister Lucy made me want to knit. She always chose beautiful wool—Candide, Lopi, Donegal. Inspired by her, I made my first sweater, a brown wool turtleneck, with my mother's help. Years later, I made a corn-yellow vest. My last big project was a pair of Red Sox red socks for my brother in celebration of the team winning the 2004 World Series. For the past few years, I have volunteered as a teacher at the Purls of Hope knitting workshop, founded by Elanor Lynn and others, at the Children's Hope Foundation in New York City. I met Elanor at Bennington College, when we were both students there. She had a distinct style, and an appreciation of vintage clothing that I shared. I was drawn to her knitting workshops because I remembered her as a very creative knitter and I wanted to volunteer somewhere.

The knitting workshop at Purls of Hope is a weekly program that teaches beginners to knit by working on small, easy-to-manage squares that are then patched together into blankets for baby strollers. We teachers cast on twenty stitches, then show beginners how to knit. As I do this, I tend to repeat Elanor's own lines—"into the back, around, down, and off"—like a ballet teacher naming the moves as they happen, in progress. The knitted "squares" are actually all shapes, sizes, and colors. Some end up looking like oblong, bean-shaped pieces; these can be particularly useful in patching together other irregular shapes and they give the finished blanket a lot of character.

The blankets remind me of Piet Mondrian's paintings, except the patchwork of offset squares is soft and wooly. The blankets, a beautiful mix of colors, knitting styles, and textures, are eventually donated to families affected by AIDS.

One night, Elanor brought up Homer's Penelope, from the Odyssey, and how she imagined her to be a knitter, not a weaver. You see, she unraveled the cloth she made each night, which would be hard to do on a loom, but all too easy if it were knitted. Penelope says:

"Young men, my suitors now that the great Odysseus
has perished, wait, though you are eager to marry me,
until I finish this web, so that my weaving will not be
useless and wasted.
This is a shroud for the hero Laertes,
for when the destructive doom of death which lays men
low shall take him,

least any Achaian woman in this neighborhood hold it
against me that a man of many conquests lies with no
sheet to wind him."
So she spoke, and the proud heart in us was persuaded.
Thereafter in the daytime she would weave at her great
loom, but in the night she would have torches set by,
and undo it.
So for three years she was secret of her design,
convincing the Achaians, but when the fourth year came
with the seasons returning,
one of her women, who knew the whole story, told us,
and we found her in the act of undoing her
glorious weaving.
So, against her will and by force, she had to finish it.

—*Homer*, The Odyssey *(Richmond Lattimore translation)*

WEAVER OR KNITTER, Penelope is one of the first women
in literature who is shown at work, making her own cloth.
Because of Elanor, I think of Penelope whenever I undo
rows of stitches (which I do every so often; on those red
socks, at least a few inches, twice). And I think of Arachne,
too, who challenged Athena, goddess of wisdom, to a weaving
contest—and lost. Arachne was turned into a spider—the
ancients thought that spiders wove their webs.

I look for nuggets like these when I study mythology and art history. I have always been interested in the origin of the details that lie on the surface, like regional dialects and accents, for example.

During my college years, I read about the fishermen's sweaters made in Guernsey, one of the Channel Islands between Devon, England, and Cherbourg, France, in the book Patterns for Guernseys, Jerseys and Arans: Fishermen's Sweaters from the British Isles by Gladys Thompson. She traveled all over Britain, stopping fishermen in the street and consulting with their wives and others, so she could get a good look at the patterns and note them down. I was so taken with the guernsey sweaters and often think of them as the ideal shape: columnar. Think of the capital above a fluted column. The capital is ornate, highly patterned at the top (shoulders, neck, chest); then comes the column itself, ribbed vertically or knitted in plain stockinette stitch.

I have never made one. I did use elements of a guernsey stitch pattern in the welt, or waistband, of the corn yellow vest I mentioned. Unknowingly, I used the "Poor Man's Wealth" pattern, which, according to Thompson, is several rows of purl knitting and was given its name because it is difficult to count—and so it is. The pattern makes rows of horizontal ribs, and I could not tell whether a purl or knit row would return me to basic stockinette.

Guernsey sweaters fit close to the body. The patterns accentuate a man's broad shoulders and then draw the eye down vertically, elongating the waist. Welt, gusset, shoulder strap, neck band . . . I think even the names of the sweater parts say that they are hard-wearing work clothes. The gussets are diamond-shaped inserts at the underarm and neck, done in a reinforcing rib stitch that allows for free range of movement. The shoulder strap is a wide, patterned band that covers the top of the shoulder from the neck to the lower shoulder. Thompson says that the sleeves are knitted from the top downward, so that when the wrists and elbows become worn they can be easily repaired. The patterns were especially intricate across the chest—more patterning, using more yarn, meaning more warmth where it mattered most, across the trunk, over the heart. I also learned that the knitter would combine distinct patterns so that the wearer would always be recognized. Patterns traveled along with the fishing fleet, and new patterns would be introduced into a community by a bride from another town.

Guernsey sweaters are traditionally made of five-ply, glossy, inky blue-black wool. This coloring reminds me of mussel shells; they seem plain black at first, but if you look closely you will see striated indigo, light blue, brown, purple, and gray. The inside of the shell is even more beautiful, smooth pearly gray holding the deep orange-yellow of the mussel. I like it when my clothes bring to mind things in nature, maybe because now I spend most of my time in the city.

Other traditional guernsey sweater colors are gray-blue—the earliest sweaters are this color—and the cream of undyed fleece. These colors are sky colors and make me think of winter and storms. Since the late nineteenth century, dyes have been mostly synthetic, aniline dyes made from coal-tar products, and I wondered where the early guernsey knitters got the dyes to color their wool. I read that the blue dye came from fermented woad leaves. Woad is a wild mustard plant: Isatis tinctoria. The active dye ingredient in woad (glucoside indican) is the same as in indigo, which also gives a deep blue-gray tint, though the two plants are not related. They don't even look alike: woad has domed clusters of tiny mustard yellow flowers atop a long skinny stem, with long pointed leaves, and indigo is bushy and has purple, pealike flowers and lots of pretty oval leaves. Indigo is native to India and Africa. In the 1770s, it crowded out the woad trade in England, and then a century later, aniline dyes replaced indigo.

I grew up in Wellfeet, Massachusetts, fifteen miles from the tip of Cape Cod. The land juts out seventy-five miles into the Atlantic Ocean. Wellfleet is unusual for a coastal town in that it has miles of beaches along the Atlantic, a harbor, miles of bay beaches, marshland, plus a dozen freshwater kettle ponds. Shellfishing provides year-round income to commercial fishermen, but tourism seems to drive the town. Many believe the best oysters come from Wellfleet. The town has, and has had for decades, an off-season population of about 3,000. In the summer it grows to 17,000.

The fishermen in Wellfleet look more like farmers, or anyone else who works outside. They wear T-shirts, flannel shirts, jeans, and whatever weatherproof gear is best at the time. There are no handmade sweaters for fishermen there, but there is a special language having to do with fish that I remember from when I was a teenager. The boys would call the girls after fish: "mud hake," or "hake" for short. Hake is a fish related to the cod. Also, "sand dab," which is a small flatfish. And "scow," for a flat-bottomed boat that carries freight and is pushed or poled along (the local definition of scow seems to be any old boat in disrepair). This is the first time I ever looked up these words in the dictionary. I looked up pictures of these things too, and was amazed to see beautiful and carefully drawn scientific illustrations of mud hakes and sand dabs. As a teen, I thought that these fish must be ugly, like the wide-mouthed goosefish I would see washed up on the beach every once in a while.

There is special language used in Guernsey making, too. The names of the stitch patterns reflect the landscape; they are things you might find in any seaside community:

• Cable or rope stitch looks like two strands of rope running up and down a sweater. Sometimes an anchor is knitted near the rope.

- Diamond shapes represent fishnet mesh; we see the raised edges of string the nets are made of.
- Herringbone is the familiar fish skeleton form. You see this pattern a lot in wool suiting material.
- Moss stitch, also called cat's teeth, hailstones, rice stitch, or birds e'en, gives a pretty pebbled effect when you knit the purl stitch and purl the knit stitch.
- Zigzag lines signify lightning or a winding footpath up steep, rocky land, and can even signify life's "ups and downs" and "marriage lines."
- Step pattern looks like the metal ladders embedded in the stone quays. The Guernsey landscape is very rocky; granite lines the coast.

Thompson's book has photographs dating back to the 1850s, mostly of fishermen wearing their guernseys. Some of the best sweaters appear as if they are carved out of wood: the detail of the relief—high and low textures—is so well defined. I think this has to do with the size of the needles (very small) and the quality of the yarn. It is tightly twisted, strong, and not stripped of its natural lanolin, so it has a beautiful luster. The oily lanolin repels water too—a further practicality.

As I remember it, for needles, knitters used lengths of stiff wire, five to eight pieces of it, pointed at both ends and up to eighteen inches long. They would knit in the round to make a cylindrical shape such as the sleeve or the body of the sweater—knitting around and around rather than back and forth over two needles—and they would sharpen the wires on their stone doorsteps. Reading this inspired me to make my own needles out of wooden dowels from the hardware store and bamboo skewers from the grocery store. Here's how:

1. Buy hardwood dowels (quarter inch are the easiest to find, but art supply stores sell smaller ones in the model-making section).

2. Saw the dowels to size (nine or more inches for double-pointed needles and much longer, about fifteen to eighteen inches, for single-pointed ones). Because they are so long, you may not have to fix a knob or wooden bead at the end to keep your stitches from slipping off, but there is always that risk!

3. Sharpen the ends with a pencil sharpener.

4. Sand the dowels very well, using coarse and then fine sandpaper. I like to use white sandpaper for this because it leaves no dark residue. Pay special attention to the tips, making sure they are evenly tapered and blunt. If they are too pointy, they will snag the yarn.

5. Rinse the needles with water to get the dust off, and then let them dry. You may want to sand them again.

6. Wax the needles with butcher's wax or any beeswax and

orange-oil mixture. Put extra wax on the tips. Leave the wax on overnight and buff it well with a soft cloth the next day. You want the needles to feel nice and smooth.

Note:

- Inch dowels make size 10 needles.
- Bamboo skewers make size 4 needles.
- English needles are sized differently—their 12 is our 2.
- Knitting wires were anywhere from U.S. size 0 to 2.

I once made about seven pairs of these needles to bring to the knitting workshop when they were running low on needles. It was good to see people working with them. They reminded me of myself when I was learning to write—we were given thick pencils because they were easy to hold. The wooden needles make a nice sound and are not as slippery as metal ones. I think this is especially good for beginning knitters. We joked about how some people, in a pinch, would get out their chopsticks and pencils and knit with those. It is this improvisation that I like. Knitting can otherwise be quite rigid and strict: all the needle sizes and gauges, the stitch counter, the lengthy instructions, the precise graphs.

At home in Wellfleet I have a bag full of undyed wool from Ireland, maybe twenty skeins of it. After writing this, I can picture the scene: get woad seeds, plant them, make dye, and dye the wool to knit the guernsey. Is it like art for art's sake? A lot of work for something I could buy? I remember my mother often said, "Don't overdo." This saying is always very comforting to me because it gives me time to reflect, to think if I really need to undertake a particular task. But my nature tells me I will be happiest if I make this woad scenario a reality. So I bought the woad seeds today from a store that specializes in items for alchemists. I may go through all the steps and make a guernsey sweater. Or I might just watch the woad plant grow.

Children's Hope Foundation
11 Park Place, Suite 1203
New York, New York 10007
212.233.5133

"Since 1986, Children's Hope has been developing innovative programs to help improve the quality of life for young people living with HIV and AIDS and their families."

Illustration by Lydia Vivante

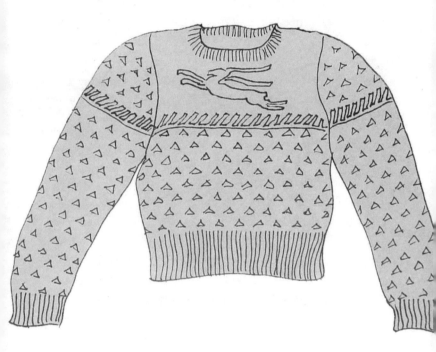

Illustration by Kathryn Alexander

FLYING STAG

by Kathryn Alexander

I live in a 150-year-old farmhouse in upstate New York. It is a house that has been added on to so many times and in so many directions that it leaves delivery people and first-time visitors bewildered, wondering which of the five doors, each with its own porch, to approach first. The house's odd footprint and multiple entryways give only a hint of what the inside holds: there are mudrooms, of course, and many neat little rooms with hallways off of them; a small room that suggests a library off a larger living room; a middle room whose earlier function I can't even imagine; a dining room with exposed, hand-hewn beams; a formal parlor with fireplace; a cozy winter room with a woodstove and comfy chairs; a large, bright kitchen with an ancient, huge, commercial-grade Garland range (two ovens, six burners, large grill). And in the midst of all this rambling quirkiness, it is one humble little bedroom that leaves the strongest impression on most of my guests.

Two staircases lead to three bedrooms upstairs. At the front of the house, one set of stairs leads to the master bedroom and an adjacent nursery that I use as an office. Toward the back of the house, the other set of stairs leads to two smaller rooms above the kitchen. The smallest and middle room, my guest room, has become the favorite of most everyone who enters it. It has all you could hope to see in a small guest bedroom: bed, dresser, rocking chair, bookcases over flowing with books. Knotted pile rugs cover most of the wide-board pine floor, an antique quilt made of silk saris covers the bed, and an assortment of vintage curtains lines the windows. I filled the room with what I imagined would make a guest comfortable. And for my own comfort, I added The Sweaters.

Lining the walls of this room are sweaters my mother knit for me and my five brothers and sisters while we were growing up in northern Wisconsin, where snow and ice abound through the winter months. Harsh as I find those winters now, as a child I saw them as a magical landscape of smooth, sparkling ice to glide across on our skates, and white, fluffy hills to slide down on skis and toboggans. Growing up, I never even thought about how wonderful it was to have a mother who knit for us; I just figured all moms knit and made really beautiful and functional clothing for their families. Boy, as a woman who knits I certainly feel differently about this now!

Red Heart was the wool yarn of choice for my mom. She got hers at the North Woods Five and Dime; it was ninety-nine cents for a four-ounce skein and often on sale for less. I loved it whenever my mom started a new knitting project because the skeins of yarn had little red metal hearts on them, and I would collect these as the skeins were made into balls; I just loved the way they looked in a little pile. I was often the human yarn swift for my mom, a hand in each end of the skein, twisting and turning, trying to keep up with her as she rolled the yarn into balls.

The sweaters that now hang on the wall range in size according to the age we were when my mom made them for us. I was six or seven when she made my sweater, and as far as I am concerned, it is the best. I love the size of it; it is so small. Also, I was a horse-crazy kid (and am now a horse-crazy adult), and the sweater is greenish blue with a white stag leaping across the yoke amidst a field of snowflakes. I imagined the stag as a flying horse skimming just above a field of dandelions gone to seed. We had lots of fields with dandelions and Indian paintbrush in them, and I rode through them daily. I also galloped a lot, and I know when my horse was flat out it must have looked just like that stag. My older brother's sweater is red, with white snowflakes as a background and two green skiers racing through evergreens on the yoke. My mother used this pattern one more time for my little brother, changing the color scheme to light blue with white skiers, trees, and snowflakes. One sister's sweater is light blue with a field of snowflakes; on the yoke is a white, V-shaped band with red hearts and large snowflakes. The other sweaters are bright turquoise, red-and-black snowflake motifs, and all have snowflakes in the background. One of them has rows of large snowflakes across the surface and lots of color and detail, not just a yoke motif.

The sweaters evoke different childhood memories for all of us, my mom included. When I asked her what she remembered when she thought about the ski sweaters, she didn't remember so much making them as us wearing them. She sees us going up the hill by way of the rope tow, and remembers hoping it would not warm up enough through the afternoon for us to want to shed our parkas. This would mean the rope we grabbed onto to go up the hill would rub on the arms and sides of the sweaters, roughing up the yarn and making the sweaters turn a dark, ugly gray. She thinks about how happy we all were, and how lucky we were that we all loved to ski and skate.

When I talk to my little brother about the sweaters, he recalls the many photos of us, all wearing my mom's knitting—not just sweaters, but scarves, hats, mittens, and even the long cable socks we wore with knickers when the ski weather warmed up a bit.

I think of the weekends spent at a little local ski hill not far from our house: coming into the lodge to warm up, having hot chocolate and a hot dog with chili for lunch and listening to music on the jukebox. Today, when I hear some of the songs that were on that jukebox, like "Mountain of Love" by Johnny Rivers, they bring me right back to that little ski hill and lodge. There are countless memories, all about growing up in a big and happy family with a mother who seemed to be knitting for us whenever she was sitting still.

My strongest childhood memory is waking up early on winter mornings, when the house was still quiet and dark, silently slipping into my clothes, padding down the hall that led from the wing where my brothers and sisters and I had bedrooms, following the smells of coffee and toast into the kitchen where my dad would be standing at the counter, the radio going, making breakfast for all of us. We would say our early morning greetings, and I would bundle up in a scarf, hat, and warm socks, all made by my mom. I would be in good company while going through this early morning ritual; Bosco, the family black Lab, would be dancing around me, her toenails clicking on the linoleum floor of the utility room, gently pushing her wet nose under my arm as I laced up my boots. Lastly, I would pull on the mittens that my dad had put out on the register for me. They would be warm and smell of hay and horses. Opening the back door, I would walk down the stairs, Bosco scurrying past to be the first to the barn. The air was so cold and dry that the snow would squeak with each step I took toward the barn. This noise would alert the horses, and as they nickered in greeting and in anticipation of breakfast, they awakened my mom's small flock of sheep. Each morning my horses would greet me by coming up and putting their muzzles in the palms of my mittened hands, a sure way to dissolve the ice that had collected on their long whiskers during the cold night. They loved these mittens as much as I did, but for very different reasons.

I do not know what feelings my guests and friends have when they walk into this room, but I do know that the sweaters make a strong impression on everyone who sees them. They are colorful and now almost vintage pieces that evoke the passing of time just in their assorted sizes, and also love, in the sense that they are so beautifully handmade and well worn. There is still mustard and cocoa on a couple of the sweaters. I could not bring myself to wash away these memories before I hung them on my wall. Rather, I left them as we last wore them as children, flying down the hill and gliding across the ice.

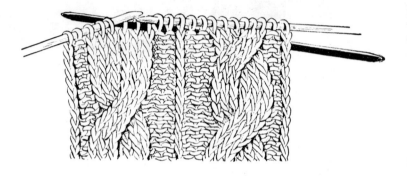

THE ORGANIC PROCESS
OF KNITTING THE WORLD

by Reine Wing Hewitt

I knit to save my soul, to protect myself from danger. During a night of energetic discussion with a friend and fellow knitter, she told me about her idea that the sweaters she knits for herself and her loved ones are a kind of armor. The idea filtered into my mind as a theory of spiritual armor: we, the creators of this armor, are accessing the guardians angels in ourselves and offering them up to protect ourselves and others.

I never doubt my instinct to create more or to keep what I need. I also give away things that I make all the time, and once they are out of my hands, they begin to fade from my memory. The idea that a person could forget the art and love they have made would upset some people, but I have always had a fading memory. This is part of what drives me to put my history into the objects that surround me.

To knit one's home is not a new idea. Birds do it, wasps do it, and I'm sure some underwater creatures that I have yet to learn about do it, too. Knitting builds my nest—or nests, as the passing of time proves is closer to the truth—but the knitting comes with me wherever I go, so perhaps the nest is always the same. Bringing the concept of home that I have honed so carefully with me everywhere seems necessary and unquestionable to me. As I am both a nester and a knitter, it is my blankets, rather than my wearables, that seem to best represent my philosophy on both knitting for the home and knitting the home itself. My space is covered in blankets, creating an encompassing and fluid softness and comfort.

A home is an imperfect place; life is imperfect. But in knitting, I cannot and choose not to aspire to perfection. I want the yarn to push me where it will, but I do have visions of what I want to create and perhaps this is why what I make I also consider to be Art. In the midst of making something I will have more visions, epiphanies of color and design. There are stories living inside me, and through my understanding of the language of knitting, I can communicate them.

Sweaters and things that require patterns, objects that are easily definable, hold no interest or sway for me. To knit, I need a night out, or the view from my rooftop, or the story of a journey I once took and can't quite remember; my fingers deftly recall things I can explain only through the language of knitting. These stories are told through colors and patterns. Their emotions can be felt in the tension of an entire section of knitting, and I can see where I was happier and where I was so angry that a square became a diamond.

I experience seasons as they relate to the weather, but perhaps more often as they relate to the joys and travails of manic depression. The seasons of manic depression are sometimes more powerful than those of the weather. In my grand moments, I can knit for hours on end, and I use that time as well as I can because I know that after each "up" there will be a "down," a time when I feel barely capable of movement. In those days and weeks, I am comforted by what I have built around me. Sometimes it is simply the knowledge of potential creation that keeps me from sinking completely. Sometimes I can knit slowly, and it is the only thing I can do. Talking and interacting with the world becomes painful and impossible in my down periods, but slowly moving colors keeps me human and alive. This is not a part of myself I am proud of, but I must accept it and try to continue on paths that at other, happier times seem so brilliantly clear. A person suffering from manic depression often looks outside the self to find the controlling or influencing factors on her condition. But I know my own patterns; they are in me. And here is where language and knitting begin to interweave for me. In my mind, the two coexist, needing no translation.

I have lately begun to think about the history of knitting, slowly coming to realize how it connects me to the history of women, to stories told and passed down through generations. Recently, I was called a feminist. The woman who made this comment meant to compliment me, but at first I could only feign an enthusiasm that came to me later, after deliberation. I went home and thought about what the woman had said. I want to be a humanist, and yet it is true that I find something deeply satisfying about being a part of a long tradition in what has most often been a woman's art form. The stigma that has in the past two decades become associated with feminism is something I need to overcome.

The history of women's rights is often associated with politics, but there is, of course, so much more to it. Knitting is a field in which women have excelled and found a language to express their intelligence, talents, and lives without words. The women who knit in this way are historians, geneologists, and lineage documentors. I am a part of all their histories, because these women are in my mind as I twist the yarn around my index finger, thinking of stories I have been told and imagining new ones.

Piles of yarn have built up around me over the years—the cast-off skeins from my mother's projects, from her friends' dead relatives, from my dead relatives, from my aunt. My friends have taken to giving me two or three balls of yarn, never the same color or kind. It is understood that they can simply pick out what they like and someday it will find its way into something that may keep them warm during some late-night sleepover. I sleep with my yarn, and it seeps into my dreams. I wake up knowing what it is that my fingers will make. I knit because it is natural and on occasion—as when it permeates my dreams—supernatural. I knit and can't remember a time before knitting.

My great-grandmother, after whom I am named, and my mother taught me how to knit. I don't remember when, but I still have the first piece I made. Hidden in a dark recess of my mother's attic is a tiny blanket made of some leftover yarn my mother gave me. There are tiny holes where stitches were lost and bulges where I added more. But I have never intended for anything I've made to look machine made. Why even try to make an object a machine can make? We are organisms, not machines.

The blanket I made in college took me four and a half years, the time it took me to graduate. The different wools are layered so the colors seem to lead into and out of each other. Because the blanket is made of wool, I could only knit when the temperature and humidity were low. I am allergic enough to wool that I itch when I knit with warm or damp fingers. This makes me conscious of every texture. I had to come up with a way to sit with all that wool I loved but could touch only in certain moments. To decide on each yarn, I would place the skeins around me, not touching me but encircling me. Rather than finding my allergy ironic, I see it as an obstacle to be overcome. As an explorer and adventurer of knitting, I see it as a challenge to be met with fortitude, and I have the unswerving desire to surpass it and overcome it.

It was during in the second year of knitting the blanket that I began to trust my cheeks. I have sometimes thought as I was riding the subway that it must look odd how I knit one row or ten and then rub the knitting against my face. This wasn't a method I came up with on my own, but something that was unintentionally passed on to me. When my great-grandmother was taken over by Alzheimer's, her hands would weave invisible yarn and then rub it on her cheek. She would speak French—a language I don't speak or understand—in pieces, and then go back to her invisible yarn. I would watch her, intrigued, trying to see what she saw, not knowing at the time what it was that I was learning from her. In moments when I could have been overwhelmed with sadness for her and her plight, I found myself entranced by imaginary yarn.

The piece I began knitting this past summer is yet another blanket. I was moving out of my apartment, and the stress of ripping apart my nest drove me to start something new. It is a collage blanket that represents the earth: seedlings, water, dirt, and growth. I began under the ground, knitting with browns and bits of green for seedlings. The next layer is one of the damp and blue-tinted earth. After the wet ground covering, the blanket begins to separate into abstract tree trunks and grass and air. Outside among the flowers, one can weed, plant, and prune, but the plants will still grow in their own way. I see myself, instead, as a gardener of yarn. This is an analogy I like, although in reality I am, sadly, a killer of plants. I don't understand plants, but with yarn I am at ease. I think this blanket will take a few more winters for me to complete, because the flow of the process of knitting waxes and wanes for me, with the weather and also my depression. Also, there are colors and textures I can already see that I will need but don't yet have.

I knit in a style I term "organic," but I don't understand how anyone could knit otherwise. I have taught some friends how to knit. At first, even before we begin, they want to know what it is they are going to make.

"What does it matter? Let your fingers learn the language; without fear, just create. Later we will think about the object, but it is really the process that is important." This is what I tell them.

The organic knitting I believe in, and on occasion come close to preaching to anyone who will listen, has a mind of its own. As with every medium I work in, my knitting is mainly directed by the materials that are made available to me in an "organic" fashion by the world. Some things I can finish in a single sitting; others take five years to complete. I have waited years to discover just the right yarn to finish a project. Although the "found" aspect of my methodology doesn't exclude buying yarn.

I like to visit knitting stores in my hometown and when I travel. I then buy what I need or what catches my eyes or fingers. Sometimes when traveling, I go intentionally without knitting materials. It then becomes my mission to find knitting stores and to meet people. When I am in a place where a language other than my own is spoken, I make it a point to learn the words necessary to shop for and discuss what I am looking for.

In Edinburgh last winter, I found the only independently owned knitting store in the city. It had snowed the night before, which is unusual in Edinburgh. So, inspired by the weather, I bought chunky yarn to make wrist warmers for myself and my hostess. I had the owner of the store teach me how to make button holes for the thumbs. This was a good and simple project that I could knit while wandering around the beautiful, mysterious, Gothic city of moody poets and mist.

What is it to live with knitting? What does it mean to live?

My philosophy is something I have yet to completely understand. Yet I know that the process must respect life and be unafraid of mistakes. If I discover that I turned my knitting around or changed my stitch, I often allow for the minor mutation. This gives the idea of "mistake" a new meaning and one that, rather than detracting from the piece, gives it new depth and is usually wonderfully subtle.

As I write this, it becomes clear to me that I knit to understand myself. Perhaps this is why patterns have never made sense to me—I knit my own ideas and feelings. I don't see the world through a veil of knitting; rather, I transcribe myself with it. It is the way I remember and grow and focus. I knit without regret. I try to live the same way, working with what I have. In both knitting and living, if I must separate them, I must think constantly about this idea and remind myself that I am part of a greater whole. I am part of a family, a culture, a species, a planet, and therefore all I create is also part of these things. My knitting and I, we are a part of history, part of the world.

MILLION DOLLAR KNITTER

by Teva Durham

I've had a few encounters with celebrities. As a New York denizen you know to expect these situations, so you try to take it in stride and act as if it's a normal occurrence. Once, at Fairway, Uma and I happened to both be reaching for a bin of snowpea pods, and she smiled—a sight that could take anyone's breath away. I let her go first, and I vowed to eat only peapods from then on. Once I babysat for DeNiro and Keitel at the same time. It's too hard to explain how that came about, but it sure was economical for them. Once, my ex-boyfriend hung out all night with Matt Dillon and Sean Penn. He phoned from a bar, promising I could join the gang, but he slouched home at noon the next day, having left his promise unfulfilled. Actually, some of my high-school friends had parents who were "in the business," and one younger class member, though not a close friend of mine, went on to become everyone's "Friend" and to marry Brad Pitt (and lose him). Yes, I went to the Fame high school, but my ambition to be an actress is now puzzling to me. How could I ever have thought I wanted that kind of attention?

I'm happiest now when I'm hiding behind my knitting needles, but I've enjoyed some public exposure. I've been granted my fifteen minutes (as Warhol said) here and there. Once, the Travel Channel picked me off the mile-long line at Henri Bendel's "open call" for new designers to film me as I showed the buyers my knits. The segment is re-aired sometimes during Fashion Week, but I had to cancel my Bendel's trunk show after 9/11, and they never renegotiated. Once, a local reporter profiled my new-age knitting class in a detailed article. I was shocked to see some of the details in print; she described me as an attractive thirty-something, long blonde hair parted down the middle with "belly eight months along and no ring on her finger." She'd never asked for my marital status or due date. Hey, so I'm not your conventional idea of a knitting teacher, but is it my fault that in this town it's hard to find a straight man who'll commit? My biggest accomplishment to date (besides the natural delivery of a ten-pound baby) and claim to fame is that I recently authored a knitting book. I can now Google myself and read all sorts of comments, but I try to avoid the temptation to do so. You never know whether what pops up will elate you or spoil your day. I felt like a rock star at my book launch when a blogger asked me to autograph her hand. The book proved the hit of the season among the stitch-'n-bitch set, though I hope its (rather than my) notoriety will last longer than fifteen minutes.

My success from the book has been exhausting, although there have been dreamy moments amid plenty of reality checks. I now have more creative opportunities than ever before, but my days begin with a race to feed, dress, and deposit my willful toddler at preschool. I'm usually sporting a disheveled look, which I could try to pass off as ragamuffin chic but for the yogurt fingerprints on my thighs. On the walk home, I clutch my bittersweet victory cup of java, already missing my daughter's constant chattering, but relieved that I managed to get her there one more time, with the patch she must wear to regain her eyesight after an injury. Suppressing the separation anxiety and ignoring the shadow cast on the day by the eye thing, I start to regain a sense of myself and plan what to tackle in the hours before retrieving her. Usually, I must finish the sleeves for a sample due yesterday, draw schematics and size patterns for samples I've turned in for magazine shoots, and print a 300-piece wholesale pattern order; basically, whatever I can get done will mean not sacrificing sleep in the wee hours.

KEEP ALL THE ABOVE IN MIND when I tell you what ensued one morning when I returned home to the usual dog-moping-on-the-floor-awaiting-his-walk and twelve fresh messages flashing on the machine. Two calls were from Diana of Make Workshop. I'd almost forgotten my commitment to teach a two-session class on my ballet tee that night and the following week. "You'll never guess who signed up for your class. You'll freak!" was the gist of both messages. Diana, a self-professed dork turned do-it-yourself fashionista, presides over a studio on the Lower East Side where classes are offered in everything from dyeing yarn to cobbling your own Manolos. She also just got a big book deal, which is good news for anyone who wants to see sewing make a comeback. As I dialed, I tried to guess who my surprise student could be. Who warranted such excitement? Maybe a fashion designer who didn't know how to handknit—I'd taught a few of those—or a model. The knitting trend has often been in the media, with celebs spotted knitting backstage at runway shows or on movie sets. Some passionate plebian knitters, from what I've gathered in online forums, feel their hobby is validated by this press while others feel the ancient craft is being usurped by fly-by-night novelty scarf knitters. And now I was to have face time with an actual knitting celebrity. Indeed, I thought, I may become responsible for whether this celeb continues to explore knitting.

Well, imagine my awe when my enrollee turned out to be Hilary Swank. "Are you sure it's the Hilary Swank?" I asked Diana. Yes, it had to be, she assured me. The actress, who'd just snagged the Oscar for that Clint Eastwood boxing film, had professed her knitting obsession on Jay Leno, plus the address on the credit card seemed about right. Actually, I'd never seen any of her performances. A friend tried to get me to go to *Boys Don't Cry*, but after reading a review, I wimped out, fearing the images would haunt me for weeks as happens to me with some powerful films. A single mother for more than three years, Pooh's Heffalump Movie is all I've seen on the big screen.

My father, who I tend to turn to in panicked states, had no idea who Hilary Swank was. This helped put things momentarily into perspective. He's retired and into the Web, so by noon—when I had every piece of my wardrobe strewn over my bed, had arranged for babysitting, and planned a hurried manicure—he'd sent a slew of links to articles about Hilary and husband Chad Lowe decorating their Greenwich Village townhouse, etc. He'd alerted my siblings, who'd all called me to fill me in on her movies. They seemed more impressed by this brush with a star than by any of the other things I'd done in my knitting life.

I emailed my editor, who is more experienced with public appearances since she's been on Martha Stewart's show. "Re: Emergency. How to Behave/Dress in Presence of Starlet. Melanie, Can you believe Hilary Swank enrolled in my ballet tee workshop? Tonight! No time for makeover.

Advice?" Melanie suggested I just act normal, acknowledge her by saying something like "I admire your work," and be sure to bring my book along to show everyone.

On the way to the subway, I popped into Sephora where I tested a delicious Gucci fragrance I can't afford. I probably won't buy it anyway, on principle, as its name is a crude summation of the fashion impulse: "Envy Me." I was becoming a bit nervous and, replacing the bottle to its narrow glass shelf, I knocked it to the floor where it shattered and splashed over my boot. Whoa, now I smelled like a gigolo on the prowl. I did some relaxation and concentration exercises on the packed and sweltering subway. I wondered if Hilary might want to be incognito, to remain anonymous lest the other students fawn over her (or post mean things about her on the Internet later). There were only six students, but Diana joked that if word got out there would be a stampede. Should I nix the round of introductions that usually start off the class? Maybe she would use an alias. What kind of knitter would she be?

When I entered the classroom, several young women were picking yarns. A crochet class was being taught at one of the tall tables, and I put out my book and samples on the other. Hilary came over and introduced herself with a firm handshake. There you go, I thought, she is used to navigating situations and knows how to put everyone at ease. She was dressed down, tomboyish in layered

T-shirts over loose khakis, hair pulled back, and without a stitch of makeup. On the street you might pass her by without taking notice. Except her skin was utterly flawless—the kind of perfection that could take gallons of water and tons of facials. And like most movie actors she possessed the chiseled, fine bone structure the camera loves and, though not totally petite, she nevertheless seemed scaled down compared to average size. Anyone who's been to Madame Tussaud's and stood next to wax replicas of the stars will know what I mean.

The room had heightened energy, a certain buzz, as everyone took in her presence while trying not to encroach too much. Hilary had actually been given one of my ballet tees, knit by a friend, and now she wanted to make one herself. All the students were intelligent, interesting, urbane, and eager to make the garment, which is knit in the round with paired increases and decreases. However, one student—I don't know how this happened—had never, ever knit before. I had an intuition I should just go with the flow; after getting the rest started, I cast on the project for her and showed her the knit stitch like it was the simplest thing (which it is).

KNITTING LINGO, HOWEVER, CAN SEEM like algebra from the perspective of someone who's not worked from patterns before. The group started to panic over the instructions, but

I handed out a drawing with increase and decrease marks and stitch numbers. I explained how the diagram used in conjunction with stitch markers makes the pattern almost foolproof. Hilary had only ever followed one or two patterns before. Actually, she'd brought some of her knitting projects to show us. One was a hat that turned out so big she was going to wear it as a tube top. The other was a sweater intended for her father. She held up a back piece in tweedy beige and brown alpaca. "If you knew my Dad," she said, "You would know this yarn looks just like him." This was so endearing, and revelatory to me. As if she hadn't accomplished enough to make her father proud, she's knitting a sweater for him too. Perhaps, no matter what we achieve, we always feel we must to do more to get that most basic love and approval we all need.

I sensed that though Hilary was very enthusiastic about knitting, she'd had very little guidance, even though she would seemingly be able to get all the help and materials she'd need. She began her dad's sweater with the intermittent help of three different yarn shops, on the three occasions when she was able to pop into yarn shops. On one of these occasions, she'd approached someone for advice, and it turned out not to be an employee but Monica Lewinski. One shop misdirected her, and now the front piece was wider than the back. No one had taught her to increase, so she'd improvised her own method. When you're as involved in the knitting world as I am, you forget what it's like on the outside. But when a fledgling knitter in my twenties, I never asked for yarn shop help and made egregious "mistakes" like sewing my first sweater together with the sleeve seams facing backward, following the tailoring of my favorite jacket. Once Hilary was among us, she had a drive to learn the "correct" way to increase and decrease. She hunkered down, elbows on the table, repeating the motions like she was trying to inhabit a role, beckoning me to watch to make sure she had mastered them. She made sure she was set for the following week and pledged that all her increase and decrease marks would align perfectly. I showed her how to unknit back a few stitches or frog a few rounds to correct anything that bothered her.

Hilary was late for the second session. I had worried she wouldn't show. I knew she probably would not have much knitting time with her busy schedule and might be embarrassed not to be as far along as the other students. If she hadn't shown up, I might've felt a bit of a failure as a teacher. Except that one student had finished her tee and started another, two students were almost done, and the girl who didn't know how to knit last week was one-third finished and had only put one increase in the wrong place. One student, who worked at a gourmet cheese shop (the first week she'd brought a selection of cheeses for us to sample), was unable to attend; her husband was graduating from sommelier school as they dreamed of one day opening a restaurant. When Hilary walked in, she was absolutely breathtaking, with a flowing mane of hair and dewy makeup. She was totally different from the low-key, casual, almost-normal person of the previous week. We were all stunned, until Diana exclaimed something we were all thinking, "God, Hilary, you movie star, you. You look gorgeous. Were you at a shoot?" Hilary had posed atop a Mercedes for an ad campaign, for which her salary would be donated to charity. She was glad to have somewhere to go afterward—our knitting class—so as not to waste the effect of hours of makeup and hair. She hated when she was all done up with no place to go except home to wash it all off. She said she had been craving the gourmet cheeses all day. Everyone knit and chatted comfortably together. Hilary graciously regaled us with some stories about her life and showed us pictures of her dogs on her cell phone. Because some hadn't finished their projects, we all agreed to meet again the following week. The students would bring food and wine to compensate me for the extra time. On her way out, Hilary struck a pose in the doorframe. "Take a good look now. Next week it'll be back to plain old me." How interesting, I thought, she doesn't mind attention.

A few days before the much-anticipated knitting party, I'd pulled an all-nighter to meet a deadline, and my daughter was home recovering from eye-muscle surgery. Diana called. Hilary's assistant had contacted her because Hilary was to fly off to a film set that week and couldn't attend. However, she was desperate to finish her tee before leaving for the three-month shoot and wanted me to help her. Diana offered to call the other students to cancel; I knew they'd be disappointed, but was the point of the additional session to hang with Hilary or to get more knitting instruction? I dialed Hilary's male assistant's number.

"Accomplice Films," a woman answered. I was startled by the familiar voice. "Um, is that you, Hilary?"

"Who's calling?"

"It's Hilary's knitting teacher," I replied.

"Just a minute, I'm on the other line. Jeffrey!" After about five minutes on hold, the male assistant came on the line to see about arrangements. Diana's space, where Hilary wanted me to meet her, wasn't open that night, and on such short notice I couldn't promise anything and would have to call back. Hanging up, I wasn't sure what I was supposed to arrange. Could I be invited to her place? Despite my utter exhaustion and the first aches of a cold or flu coming on, I was scrambling to figure out how to accommodate her. I was touched that she felt it important to knit the tee; I didn't want her to have any regrets or completion issues.

I called my mom to see if she could babysit. "Don't give in to celebrities. They always want special treatment. Why don't you just say she can drop by your place so you don't need babysitting?"

"I'd have to have a total renovation or at least a cleaning service to invite her. She had a top decorator do her townhouse. My apartment is awful."

"Nonsense. Your apartment is lovely and lived in." Sure, the clutter of toys, the wall of yarn, my massive long-haired dog dominating the sofa, toddler scribbles on the kitchen walls.

"Well, take Olivia in the stroller and meet her at Starbucks or somewhere."

Does a celeb dare sit down at Starbucks? I can see the caption on page six of the Post, "Million Dollar Knitter," with a photo of radiant Hilary, holding my ballet tee on circular needles, and unidentified companions: a disheveled mother sneezing into tissues, and a strapped-in, indignant toddler with a bloodshot, puffy eye. But maybe they'd mention my book, Loop-d-Loop. Or maybe I could have a future as a celebrity knitting coach if I pulled myself together. Racked with guilt and indecision, I lay down to join Olivia, who was already napping. After a few minutes, I came up with an idea. I called Carrie, an avid knitter with a great personality, who has made at least three of my tee shirts since taking my workshop. Carrie owed me a favor since I had introduced her to Melanie, who then commissioned some designs. And it was hardly a difficult favor to ask her to help Hilary Swank. Carrie was free that night and totally psyched. Then I called Jeffrey to offer Carrie in my place, detailing her qualifications.

"Carrie and Hilary will totally get along," I prodded him, perhaps with too much hard sell. "Carrie has cute little dogs too."

Apparently, Carrie was never called back. I'm wondering if I should follow up to see if Hilary is back from location. Any advice?

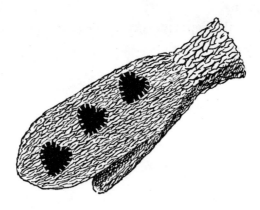

Silent Communion

by Robert Bruce Cowan

Knitting had not been going on that long. It had not happened that frequently. Its bursts had not even been that intense. It had not resulted in products that were aesthetically displeasing, nor was I unmoved by the sense of generosity that came with them, the love put into them. But somewhere along the line, knitting caused resentment.

A tyrannical, ringletted blonde who is about two and a half feet tall rules our home. She is two years old. This perfect creature is a tornado, centrifugally vacuuming in all of our attention and energy, and centripetally, often unintentionally, casting out destruction, and, of course, joys. She blows siroccoes of wonder at us, till the miraculous sand sticks in our teeth. But respite from such nourishing and terrible winds adds special weight to the time my wife and I spend together, alone.

My wife says that knitting entered her family "out of a void." That is to say, her mother, herself a child of a bitter woman with nothing creative to give, managed to learn from her nevertheless and to pass it on. My resentment also grew out of a void, or rather out of paucity, a paucity of shared downtime. It may also have come from the fact that I am not the one doing the knitting. Resentment's intrusion into the knitting activities in our household is a recent development, but resentment is a quality that can rear its unsightly head, unbidden, at almost any moment, if one isn't vigilant.

Often resentment can be effortlessly staved off. Silently sharing a room, she knitting, I reading, the world feels so right, so recentered. But sometimes, knitting means absence. I realize I've read the paragraph in my book more than once. I've struggled to pay attention because I have sensed the almost imperceptible movement of disappearance. Until suddenly, I glance up from the couch to the chaise longue, and, in her concentration, she's vanished. Resentment grabs me around the neck from behind, standing atop the radiator, and I wrestle, trying to remember that she may be gone, she may have left me all alone, but she's in a better place now, a knitting place. I should see these moments coming, and yet they creep up on me.

When she comes home from the knitting shop—where I know she's gone, even if she doesn't tell me, because her errands took two hours longer than they normally would have—she leaves a trail of glee from the car, through the mudroom, kitchen, and dining room, to the chaise where she holes up, cross-legged, in a sphere of attention about three feet in diameter, impenetrable to all but the Perfect Tornado and the rambunctious kitten. When yarn she's ordered online from some idiosyncratic, small-batch producer arrives, and she gallops in encouraging me to drool over it as she does, I know a new project has begun. When she thunders downstairs, knitting book in hand, having figured out some purling puzzle, the bell tolls. I know our time together is ticking away. I'm not sure what "a stitch in time saves nine" means, but it seems to have to do with creating more time out of less, and I'm sure that this sewing proverb has some equally vague and insidious knitting counterpart.

Now my wife is not someone who begins seventeen projects at once, each of which ends its ephemeral life when it is frustratingly demoted to the basket of unfinished . . . yarn things. She usually knows exactly what she's going to make, gets the yarn for it, and plows through it in just a few days—at least that's how it seems to me, on a good day. On a bad day, however, it feels like the second the Perfect Tornado is asleep, my spouse swan-dives into the pool of merino, or whatever it is, not to emerge for a week. On a bad day, when that yarn crosses the threshold, I know the house isn't big enough for the both of us, particularly when you add in the P.T., the dog, and that kitten. By batting around yarn that is in use, or even that which isn't, the kitten provides a sort of playful revenge and yet prolongs the activity by rudely interrupting its progress. I'm sure, though, my wife feels that she only gets to spend a little time knitting on sporadic evenings and relishes that communion.

Once upon a time, I would accompany my wife to a lot of knitting shops, only moderately interested in the endeavor but appreciative of her enthusiasm. In New York, L.A., Florida, Vermont, I found the women (for it is primarily women) who run and hang out in yarn shops to be consistently impressive in their generosity. I still go occasionally and am reminded that I've been offered everything from chocolate croissants to local beer, have made profound connections with myriad groggy pooches, and fondled yarn of such transporting texture as to be borderline erotic. My favorite stuff is from Japan—not the weird, frilly, flashy stuff that we saw so much of in San Francisco; the super simple, subtle stuff with which you could make plain garments that actually have whole universes of variation within them. That's what I like. I don't like the complex Norwegian patterns that remind me of what was popular when I was in high school, or those Peruvian sweaters in which the yarn is so coarse it feels like there are pieces of bark purposely woven into the fabric. But comfortable pieces in which the yarn speaks as much as the knitting. It doesn't say, "Look what I've become." It says, "Look what I already was and continue to be."

I have to admit that sometimes both the yarn and the idea of knitting are seductive. There is a certain spirituality inherent in a hand made product. Like a wooden bowl or a ceramic pitcher, a hand-knit garment is, in a sense, a beautiful tool, a practical creative work. I come from a family that values the practical but, in its own way, also appreciates the beautiful. It is from this dual perspective that knitting makes pragmatic sense and has ineffable meaning to me. I think that my wife appreciates the product, particularly when it is a sweater or a poncho for the Windy One. The process, however, may be what is most compelling about the whole endeavor for her: a cross between a math problem, sculpting, and walking mediation (although she does it sitting cross-legged).

Perhaps my wife's apparent disappearance is an illusion of mine. Knitting may be the activity during which she's in fact the most focused, the most present. Perhaps there isn't any anthropomorphic demon threatening me from the radiator. Perhaps I need to remember that sometimes the world seems very much at peace when I'm puttering, NPR is murmuring in the other room, we each have a Scotch on the rocks going, and she is knitting. I just need to glance up periodically to make sure she's still there.

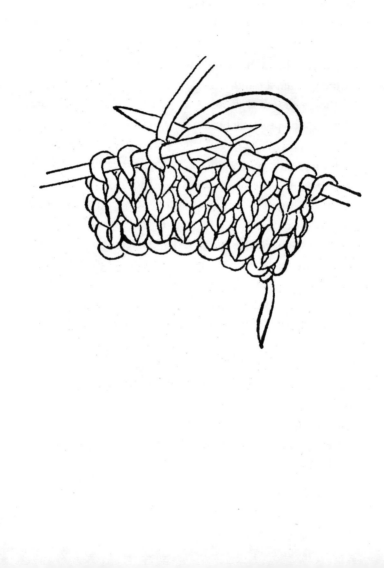

KNITTING FOR A LIVING

by Lily M. Chin

"Be careful what you wish for," the saying goes. "It might come true." This axiom can most certainly be applied to me. I knit for a living. Many think this is an enviable position. I once thought it would be an enviable position, too, imagining that I'd get to sit and knit all day, and have all kinds of yarn at my disposal for free. I'd actually get paid for doing what I enjoy most. I'd even earn name recognition amongst my fellow knitters. But I wasn't aware of the realities of turning an avocation into a vocation. These days, I love quoting a former vice president and creative director of a U.S. yarn company, which pretty much sums up the reality of my career: "Your hobby is my business."

I think some people have romantic visions of what it's like to be able to knit all day; this is their ideal bliss. They think they'd get to sit and knit all day and have all kinds of yarns at their disposal for free. They like the notion of actually getting paid for doing what they enjoy most. Some imagine they'd even earn name recognition amongst their fellow knitters. But when knitting is your job, wanting to knit something is very different from having to knit something. How often have any of us tired of a project that we did not want to continue? How often is a deadline mutable or forgiving? How often is a forced march fun?

I am often jealous of the typical hobby knitter, who can put down projects at will and not have to deal with them when they do not want to. The hobby knitter does not necessarily have to complete a project on a particular schedule. Sure, there might be a birthday coming up, or a graduation, or the holidays, and gifts for these occasions might need to be finished within an allotted amount of time. However, much is forgiven by friends and relatives when they receive a belated present, especially if it's one that's been made by hand. Additionally, a hobby knitter need not be concerned by the budget constraints of magazine and book publishers, which stipulate that if a project is not completed by a particular date, the thousands of dollars earmarked for a photographer and models will be forfeited. Their names will not be mud in the eyes of their employers. It's a lot of pressure.

This pressure means that I work under constant deadlines. Luckily, I am the type of person who thrives on pressure; it can motivate me, and I usually like challenges. I have bouts, though, when I pull all-nighters, sometimes for days, to get something finished. At times like these, I feel like I have no life outside knitting. Dinner with friends, art openings, a night at the movies with my husband, and myriad other family and social functions, all fall by the wayside because of deadlines. I call it the Cinderella Syndrome—Lily can't go to the ball; she has to stay at home and knit.

I can count on one hand the number of hand-knit or hand-crochet designers in this country who actually earn a true living wage from designing full time. I think I could probably make more money as a receptionist in an office. But if all I wanted from my career was to make money, I would have pursued math and science—the track I was on in college, when I studied chemistry and thought about a career in pharmaceuticals. Besides, I don't feel that the world of knitting and crocheting owes me a living; for better and for worse, I chose this work and this life.

I do what I do for the love of the craft. I have a tactile compulsion about yarn. I obsess about knitting and crocheting; I think about them night and day, and I am constantly coming up with ideas about them. There isn't anything I'd rather be doing. But in order to make some semblance of a viable livelihood, I work (on average) sixteen- to eighteen-hour days, seven days a week. I supplement my designing with teaching, writing, and making samples for manufacturers and ready-to-wear designers. I also develop fabric concepts for the garment industry. Many other knitters and crocheters I know design for the hand-craft market on the side. I guess I'm luckier than some, not as lucky as others. One colleague is a part-time nurse as well as a designer, another was a florist. Still other designers are married to high-earning spouses, so their income from designing can function merely as a supplement. There is only one fellow designer I know of, an unmarried woman on her own, who, before taking a salaried staff position with a major yarn company, managed to earn enough from the designing business to do it full time. She had my utmost admiration.

When trying to meet tight deadlines, I typically put in a three to four day marathon. Inevitably, I catch myself nodding off from time to time; I splash my face with cold water, brew another pot of coffee, and I'm off again. My dear, sweet husband helps a great deal. He's an architectural writer and editor, and he tells me that architecture students go through something similar in a charette—a project in which everyone works together to solve problems—where they may work straight through for days.

The most outrageous deadline I ever had was when my husband and I lived in Washington DC in 1988. I had to get a package out on a Sunday (the main post office was open, and if I got it there by 5:00 P.M., the package would arrive Monday morning) for a New York–based crafts magazine.

I began work on the jacket on Thursday and worked nonstop until I left for the post office at 4:30 P.M. on Sunday. Clifford, the spouse, literally had to spoon-feed me so I could keep working. I kid you not, he cooked, he cut up my food into bite-sized chunks, and he fed me with a fork. Then he cleaned me up.

I was sewing up seams on the jacket when he dressed me as well, as if I were a baby. He got my socks and shoes on, then looked for a box to mail the jacket in. He hailed a cab as I wove in the ends. In the taxi, I sewed on buttons, and he filled out the shipping label. He got in line at the post office as I taped up the box, and we made it to the counter just as the truck was about to pull out. Whew! Moral of the story: for those mourning the lack of time to knit, train family members to work as your production team.

Here's a blow-by-blow account of a week in my current life, the real inside story on what it's like to live with knitting, when you knit for a living:

MONDAY, JULY 2

I return from teaching in California to find yarn for a magazine's winter-issue vest project waiting for me. I'm way too exhausted to start on it, as it's late evening and I've already put in a full day's travel. But I skein up the balls in preparation starting at around midnight and go to bed close to 1:00 A.M.

TUESDAY, JULY 3

I begin swatching for the project, a unisex vest. The yarn that was sent to me—a cornflower blue sport weight—is radically different from the double-knitting to worsted weight I'd submitted my original idea in. I try knitting with the sport-weight yarn doubled. Blegh. The resulting swatch is clunky, to say the least. Not only are the stitches muddled, the weight of it is just too bulky to be elegant and practical. I heave a sigh and begin swatching on minuscule needles, working out two new swatches using a single strand of the yarn. My hands hurt, but the swatch results are magnificent: the stitch definition really pops and the lighter-weight fabric is far more refined, with better drape. I block one swatch, scan it, and e-mail it to the editor for approval.

The editor approves the newly gauged swatch at about six stitches per inch. I consider shooting myself.

I speak on the phone with a yarn company that's commissioned eight projects from me. They want them all finished in two-and-a-half weeks' time. I prepare to shoot myself.

I start to drift off around 2:30 A.M.

WEDNESDAY, JULY 4

I chart out and graph the vest in the new gauge and begin knitting on size 3 needles. Luckily, it's only a vest, not a sweater, or worse, a coat. I rent *Quills* and *Traffic* to keep me going as I begin on the back.

One of my knitter helpers called a few days ago to report that she is available to work for me. "This is during the Fourth of July holiday?" she asked. What holiday? I finally hit the pillow around 4:00 A.M.

THURSDAY, JULY 5

I receive more yarns from the yarn company I am doing the eight projects for.

I receive a postcard from another yarn company, saying they are sending yarn for what I'll call Vest Number 2, for another magazine's winter-issue vest project. Luckily, I teach only twice this month.

Tens of thousands of stitches and more than 200 rows later, the back of Vest Number 1 is complete. I begin the front while viewing *Oh Brother, Where Art Thou* and *After Night Falls*. The latter is a tad difficult to knit to, as I occasionally have to read subtitles (even living in New York all my life, my Spanish isn't that good). I get a snooze in as the sun is coming up around 5:30 A.M.

FRIDAY, JULY 6

I begin swatching for two of the eight yarn-company projects, as the original yarns I worked the ideas out in have been substituted—apparently, they wanted to feature different yarns in their line other than the ones I chose. Luckily I am still using the prescribed yarn for the rest of my pressing deadlines, so there is no need to reswatch those; I can just take the gauges off my design-submission swatches.

I get working gauges after blocking the swatches.

I finish Vest Number 1, but it still needs to be blocked, assembled, trimmed, etc. My husband gets up at 7:00 A.M., and we play "tag team" for the mattress.

SATURDAY, JULY 7

I chart out and graph the Man's Sweater and the Cabled Woman's Tunic and the Wrap around 2:00 P.M. I begin work on the first as I resort to mindless girl-power flicks: *Miss Congeniality* and *Charlie's Angels*. At 11:30 P.M., I finish the back and half the front of the Man's Sweater. Pretty fast work—I'm using size 10.5 needles. I can't believe I am actually getting some shut-eye by midnight.

SUNDAY, JULY 8

I finish knitting all of the Man's Sweater, including the sleeves, but it needs blocking, assembling, and all the rest, which I do while watching *Wonder Boys* and *Almost Famous*.

My video store loves me.

I begin the Wrap, get half of it done (I'm really glad it's on size 15 needles). My hands are aching and sore. I don't even bother going to sleep at this point.

MONDAY, JULY 9

I finish the Wrap. Luckily, no assembly is required, but I will have to block it. I diddle on the computer for some diversion, needing it after such an intense period of knitting. I will begin Cabled Woman's Tunic on size 10 needles tonight. Hmmmm, what shall I rent?

I plan on letting my knitting assistant, Joann, do the knitting on the Buttonless Jacket. The Crocheted Hat and the Crocheted Shawl are basically finished, completed sometime in the middle of the night, during a lull. But I haven't even begun the pattern writing and sizing, all of which must be done for the pieces and turned in at the same time. I also have a Twin Set to think about (worsted and sport-weight yarns, maybe I'll hire someone else to knit it). I'm still waiting for the yarn for Vest Number 2, which needs to be completed in another three weeks.

Perhaps it's not surprising after all that work, but I suffer from separation anxiety when it comes time to give away the fruits of my labor. When I send a finished project to a magazine or a manufacturer or a pattern or yarn company, I'll probably never see it again. I've invested so much time in creating something; it's totally consumed me. It's not unlike being in a doomed relationship. Tragically, inevitably, we must break up and go our separate ways—the project and I are like star-crossed lovers. Maybe this is just a tad melodramatic and sentimental, but I do often feel like my children are leaving me.

The sick thing is, when I'm not knitting for business, I also knit for my own pleasure. When I'm not traveling for business or teaching across the continent, I travel a lot for pleasure too, and that's when I knit for myself. I make things for me to wear, since I hardly ever see my commissioned projects again—everything from dresses and skirts to cardigans and accessories. I often remake the things I get published, just to have my own version. More often than not, however, I wind up making things that are less "sell-able" or "commercial," more wacky or over the top. The more off-the-wall and artsy pieces speak more closely to me and my personality. I also make gifts for my family members, like pullovers and shawls and afghans. But I always follow the same design process that I do when I'm knitting professionally: I swatch, measure gauge, chart it out, the works. Every once in a blue moon, I may indulge in the luxury of (gasp) actually following someone else's pattern and turn my brain off. Most people do something other than work to "get away from work." I just do more of it in my "spare time." Hmm, what's wrong with this picture? I guess I really do enjoy what I do for a living, despite my griping, and I want to do it all the time.

Knitting and crocheting may be my livelihood, yes, but they are also my joy. I still feel that same thrill when I start a new venture, and the thrill of realized potential when I put yarn to needles. I still get inspired when I see brick patterns on buildings or woven textures in fabrics and textiles, things that in my life and work are translated into knits. Creating something with my hands still sings to my spirit.

Most of all, sharing my passion with other knitters and crocheters who want to work up my designs gives greater meaning to my life. I actually feel useful—I've helped others to create as well, and I like knowing that my vision may have inspired the vision of others.

I've been at this for a very long time, since the age of eight, I think. I still find it fascinating that one can mold string into three dimensions with just some sticks or a hook. I find it empowering to be able to sculpt shapes to my specifications. I am mesmerized by the movements and actions of my hands. My very first design was published back in 1981, when I was in college. It was for a monthly women's magazine, a roll-brimmed hat with matching clutch purse. And in 2005 I started my own line of yarns and patterns, the Lily Chin Signature Collection—I am proud to say that I am the first American hand-knit designer to have my name on a branded label. For all the hard work, sleepless nights, hand cramps, general anxieties, and social sacrifices, I've committed myself to a life of knitting. I guess I'm in it for the long haul.

Marian's Legacy

by Jennifer Brown

Upstairs in the cedar-lined storage closet in my bedroom, taking up a lot of space, I keep two handmade, stretched out, slightly faded, oatmeal-colored fishermen's wool sweaters. I don't wear them often—they're pretty impractical unless I'm headed out to a very cold place, but when I've worn them in past winters, I've barely been able to get my coat on over them. When I did manage to get both the coat and a sweater on, the combination bulked me up so much that I couldn't bend my arms.

The sweaters are knit from thick wool, in a cable pattern that bulks them up even more. They don't match many of my other clothes—they're very L.L. Bean, and my style is less outdoorsy and more simple and black, and I rarely wear light-colored clothing above the waist. I'm terrified I would drip red wine on these sweaters, irreparably staining them.

These are two articles of clothing, however, that will never see a yard-sale table or a rack in a used-clothing store, at least not in my lifetime. My maternal grandmother, Marian Tuttle, knit them for herself and for my grandfather, Richard Tuttle, around the time I was born. Both my grandparents are gone now, but I was fortunate to know them for a good number of years—I was a teenager when my grandfather passed away, and well into my twenties when my grandmother died. Their sweaters are a remarkable reminder of these two people, warm and well worn, comforting and familiar, just as my grandparents were to me in my life.

Marian and Dick were children of the Great Depression and were married in September 1934. She worked briefly for a dentist, while he made his way up the ranks at the Bank of New York, eventually becoming a vice president. They had a close relationship before they had children, and they remained loving to each other for the rest of their fifty-plus years of marriage. They were the grandparents who demonstrated affection to each other in public and didn't mind if we saw them hugging. My grandfather's pet name for Marian was "Hunky," and he delighted in surprising her with jokes and silly pranks. She was more reserved, but always called his name with a depth and warmth that few other people could elicit. They made a home in her hometown in Westchester County, raising three daughters there. Dick was an active member of their church, singing in his bass voice in the choir. He commuted on the train twice a day, into the city and then home again. Most days, when the afternoon train came into the station,

Marian would be waiting for him on the platform, having walked from the house to meet him.

Marian was an avid knitter in the late 1960s, part of the 1970s, and into the early 1980s. She made countless slippers, mittens, and gloves for local church bazaars. Her mother, Arminda, was not only a knitter, but she also crocheted and did tatting—with Arminda lie the beginnings of the woven arts that spill down through the generations in my family. From what I have gathered from studying the patterns Marian collected and used, and her leftover skeins of yarn, she created mostly complicated cable-knit sweaters for her husband, her daughters and their husbands, and for my older cousins, all in classic khakis and heather greens. Marian was a frugal woman, and family lore has it that she started knitting sweaters after a visit to Maine to see my aunt and uncle, when she saw how much the cabled sweaters at L.L. Bean cost. I was given her patterns and yarn after she died; my aunts and mother thought of me when they were going through Marian's things, as I was just starting my own experiments with knitting.

I keep Marian's patterns in an old plastic bag, along with patterns she clipped from magazines and her notes on customizing the patterns to whomever she was knitting for. Seeing her handwriting reminds me of the older woman she was when I knew her the best—the writing is still legible, but scratchy. The torn, folded, coming-apart books that hold patterns for the children's sweaters Marian made are vintage 1970s, with the models wearing checkered pants, bulky cable knits, and floppy messenger hats.

I don't know if I'll ever use her leftover yarn, because there isn't enough of one color to complete any pattern that I work with. It is a muted kaleidoscope of browns, oatmeals, tans, and dark greens. There is also a quantity of bright orange, perhaps thrown in as a joke, but I think that must have come from someone else's collection. Having the yarn around, though, reminds me of Marian's craft, of her skill with needles, of her sweaters and hats that we grandchildren all wore, pieces passed down from one grandchild to the next. It reminds me of a time when people knit for a purpose, rather than because it was the newest fad. It's from a time when women learned these types of homemaking skills from their mothers and grandmothers instead of paying strangers to teach them. Sorry to say, I'm a woman who learned to knit from friends at a time when it was the thing to do. But I like to think that some talent has been passed down to me, that Marian's spirit guides my fingers, smoothing the wool as I work. An experienced knitter once told me that it was unusual to see a beginner thread yarn through their fingers the way I do. I must have learned it somewhere, perhaps even from watching Marian knit when I was a child.

It's comforting for me to have the patterns and the yarn and the sweaters that Marian made, because they are a physical representation of love from a woman who was not overly demonstrative in her love with many people. The time and effort she put into each piece was a huge commitment on her part. The patterns are complicated, and I see them as her way of showing her love for the recipients of her gifts. The materials are yarn from a time when everything wasn't mass produced and packaged, from a simpler time than today. It's material that has been enriched with lanolin—it is heavy, special, rich. My little-girl memory of Marian knitting doesn't give me much to go on in terms of what exactly Marian was making or for whom. But I do remember her sitting and knitting and taking part in conversations without ever looking at what her hands were doing. She knew the patterns by heart and could carry on with her fingers flashing through the wool.

Marian taught at least one of her three daughters, my mother, how to knit when my mother was in her teens, but neglected to teach her about gauge. While she was in college, my mother made her then-boyfriend, the man who would eventually become my father, a gray sweater. She knit and knit and knit. Then she brought the sweater home to show her mother and father before she gave it to her boyfriend. She thought it was a little large, but wasn't sure. My grandfather took the sweater and disappeared into his bedroom (he and my father were about the same size—very large and tall). When my grandfather came out, the sweater fit him perfectly, and he modeled it, turning this way and that. Then he turned around. He had bunched the sweater to make it fit, and it fell in folds behind him, like an elephant with too much skin. Of course, I wasn't there to witness this firsthand, but from what I hear, the laughter continued for hours. My grandmother, in her skilled and thrifty way, unraveled the giant-size sweater that my mother had labored over for so long and made three new sweaters: one for my grandfather, one for my mother's boyfriend, and one for my cousin, who was then a little boy. Three sweaters from the original one. That's how big it was. And my mother never wanted to see another skein of gray yarn again.

This story is precious to me for so many reasons: for the innocent, loving, earnest efforts of my mother; for the supportive yet practical jokester role of my grandfather; and for my grandmother's waste-not, want-not solution in fixing things for everyone. It functions as a sort of snapshot of these people and the positions they have always held in my life, a perfect example of who they were deep inside.

My grandmother's family had a history of mental illness, and Marian did not escape the sickness. She was injured in a car accident that left her with whiplash, necessitating that she remain very, very still for extended amounts of time in order to heal herself. My theory is that she got a little too much inside her own head during these still times, enabling the depression that ran rampant through her family to take hold. She didn't knit for some years in the early 1970s—they certainly would not allow metal knitting needles or any other sharp objects in the mental hospital where she was confined and treated on and off for years. I was just a baby during this time, so I don't remember it, but I know that it was a very dark period for our family. I have heard stories about family members going to visit Marian in the hospital, finding her a shell of her former self after shock treatments. And I've heard stories about how, when my grandfather brought her home, Marian just blankly sat there. She hardly knew who she was, let alone the patterns of her knitting.

My grandfather was a stoic man who lived through this very unhappy time with a sick wife he loved very much but could do nothing for, and so to him—and so for the rest of us—her illness was a verboten subject; he refused to hear anyone talk about it. We did not mention her shock treatments, only said that she had been "sick" and had had "a bad case of whiplash." This was the age of nonacknowledgement: "If I don't talk about this, then it didn't happen," before the era of shared feelings. Marian herself never gave much credence to her mental illness, although she remained on antidepressants for the rest of her life. I don't know if she missed knitting while she was in the hospital, if her hands missed the familiar, soothing motions of the needles. I know that severely depressed people can lose sight of the things that are important to them, and I think this is probably why she didn't knit for so many years after her release.

She also didn't knit much when she lived with my parents, from 1990 until her death in January 2002. She had too many other things to take care of: reading the New York Times, playing bridge, going for her evening walk, watching her favorite political programs, and cocktail hour at 5:00 p.m. I'm not sure why she moved on from her knitting hobby, but from the time she lived with us until shortly before her death, a span of over a decade, she did not knit.

We all knew in the backs of our minds that something was up in November 2001 when Marian picked up her needles again and started casting on. It was a return to what may have been a happier time in her life, before her depression. It may have been a retreat from the world, in light of the recent 9/11 upheaval at home and abroad. We didn't know what she was starting. She didn't know either; when asked, she had no answer. I wonder if it was just a turning back to another pattern in her life: the feeling of the wool between her fingers, the familiar muted clack of the metal against itself, the progression as she wove back and forth, just using her hands again in that way. She may have known that her life was drawing to a close, and before she went perhaps she wanted to remember that feeling of making something wonderful, something to keep her loved ones warm and cozy, a return to something she knew she did with extraordinary talent. She went for a visit to my aunt's house over Christmas, became ill almost overnight, and made it home to die, in her own bed as she had hoped she would, on January 2. The project she was knitting died with her. I don't know what became of it; I don't recall seeing it after Thanksgiving.

In addition to those matching oatmeal-colored sweaters Marian made over three decades ago for herself and my grandfather, I also have a photo of the two of them from the late 1970s, wearing the sweaters. In it, my grandmother is the recipient of a bear hug from my grandfather, her smaller frame lost in his bulk, against an autumn background. They both look genuinely happy, secure, and warm. There is no indication of their troubles with my grandmother's illness. They look like an Everyman grandmother and grandfather. They are smiling.

When my grandfather died, fourteen years before Marian, I chose his sweater as a memento of him when my grandmother was cleaning out his closets. I liked to wear it then because it still smelled of his Bay Rum aftershave and sandalwood soap. I was in high school at the time and wore it when I could, on walks in the autumn and spring, when I needed something a little warmer. Almost twenty years later, I think I can still detect those special smells when I hold the sweater close, even though it has been worn countless times and carefully washed and dried. I also wore it through college, on visits to the ocean in the fall and apple picking with friends, and into adulthood when it was something to keep at the office in case the air conditioning was too cool. It was scratchy but comforting, like a hug from a grandfather should feel. I could almost hear his laughter when I wore it, remember what it felt like to wrap my arms around his barrel of a chest and give him a hug. When Marian died, I was asked to help clean out her closets. I chose only that matching sweater of hers to keep. Her other clothes were dated and much too small, but this piece of her would fit me perfectly. And I thought it only right that her sweater be joined with his.

I learned to knit later in life, and right before my daughter was born, I finished my first sweater for her, which is tiny in comparison to my grandparents' sweaters that reside in my closet. Made of soft alpaca, it is relatively simple against the trickier cables and patterns that flowed from Marian's hands. Still, I see it as an artifact of my family, past and present, and when my daughter has outgrown her sweater, it will go into the closet with those of her great-grandparents. As will the sweaters made by Marian for my parents, which I have been informed I will also inherit. This physical representation of someone who is no longer alive is important in a simple way; the sweaters came from the hands of a person who cared enough to spend the time making things that were so valuable in their beauty and function.

I regret that it wasn't Marian who taught me this art that she was so skilled at. I hope that my daughter will want to learn how it's done, when she is ready. My mother knits again—but not with gray yarn—and I continue with blankets and hats for friends and their babies, a scarf for my husband of hand-spun indigo-blue wool. Someday, I will attempt an adult-sized sweater, and I will try to follow one of Marian's patterns. I hope when I am gone, that my granddaughter or great-granddaughter will know the history behind all the family's sweaters and how knitting has been woven through our family for generations.

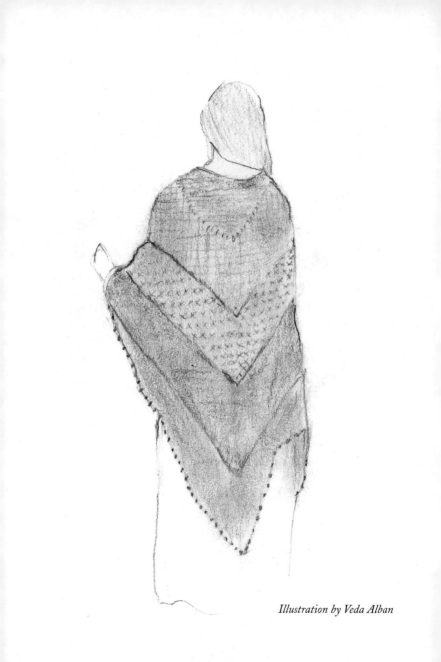

Illustration by Veda Alban

BLACK IS THE COLOR

by Veda Alban

We were on the train from Washington DC to New York. There were hundreds of us, mostly college students returning home for the Thanksgiving holiday, crammed three and four to a seat, straddling suitcases in the aisles, and crouched in inconceivably small spaces not meant for birds or mice, let alone passengers. Someone was playing a radio, and we, the ragged crew, hummed, sang, and tapped to the rhythm, and talked about exams and dates and hopes for the future. The afternoon fall sun filtered through grimy windows, playing its aimless games with the cigarette-smoke-filled interior. The cars carried their own odors beyond the smoke: spilled soda soaked into the cracked and scarred linoleum of the floors; bubble gum; body heat scented with remnants of cologne; and the pervasive aroma of hot metal and soiled vinyl. Shortly before our arrival in New York, the train bucked once, then jolted to a halt. The din that had presided became a hush through which a voice, somewhere between a moan and a scream, was heard: "No, oh my God." In that second all sound and motion froze. The year was 1963, and John Fitzgerald Kennedy had just been shot.

Except for an occasional murmur of disbelief and horror echoing the permanence of change impacting our lives, we were left speechless; all attention focused on the radio

with its continuous news updates etching vivid images in our minds. We stared blankly at one another, hoping to see on some other face the comprehension we lacked. The silence was infused with our youthful hope, defying us to believe our president was mortally wounded.

Beyond this, I have not much recollection. I do remember that there was a palpable pain in the hollow place that had been my heart and when my feet touched the pavement in New York City's Pennsylvania Station, tears that I thought might never cease obscured my vision. Bags in tow, I threaded my way through streaming tight rows of pedestrians until, several blocks from the station, their numbers thinned and I found myself in more open spaces. In less than an hour, I stood in front of my parent's town house.

I paused at the door with a sense of excited anticipation at the prospect of seeing my parents, and also dread, due to an overwhelming feeling of being an outsider in my own family. There wasn't much sympathy for my grief at home and certainly no solace, since my mother and father felt that JFK had earned his assassination. My brother—my

friend and my only ally—was not at home for the greater
portion of the Thanksgiving holiday that year. He was
beginning to carve out his own private life apart from the
rest of us, and, while I was glad for him, I missed his support and the opportunity to share ideas with a like-minded
individual. Bereaved and lost, I paced and ate and jogged
the city streets without relief. Before long, my behavior was
driving my parents crazy, so my mother suggested I sit
down and "chill out"—her exact words, uttered in an
attempt to be modern.

At the time, she was knitting a tangerine-colored
sweater. I desperately wanted it to be for me; it was a color
my mother had always said was my color, so I dared to hope
for a while, and I could see myself wrapping its warm softness around me. My mother had always prided herself on
being "busy," but what that meant to her escaped me
because she had no hobbies and certainly had never made a
gift for any of us in the family. She hadn't ever seemed
artistic to me; I hadn't even known that she was a knitter.
But now that I had discovered her secret, I begged her to
teach me.

All the women in my dormitory had two hobbies, it
seemed. One, they played bridge and had taught me the
basics. Sad to say, most of those tedious lessons, having
been mentally identified as foreign agents, were exiled to
the appropriate region of my brain for elimination. The

women's other hobby was knitting. They created beautiful, intricate sweaters, scarves, and coverlets for their beds. They sat curled in feline poses, gabbing away, sometimes playing bridge and . . . knitting. I was an outsider to this art form and envious. Several times I had come close to asking them to teach me, but no good opportunity presented itself. But now I wanted to knit because I wanted a distraction— something to fill the idle, lonely hours at home and something tangible to hold on to when I left whatever vestiges of security existed there. I wanted something permanent.

My mother did not look forward to teaching me to knit—we did not have a history of successful interactions. She had never let me forget that she had failed in her efforts to teach me to read a dozen or so years ago. She had dubbed me "impossible" then and washed her hands of any further education of me. For my part, allowing her to teach me something was a real exercise in trust. Feeling dragged down by emotion at the prospect of our lessons, I was determined to prove her wrong in her thinking of me, or at least to have the satisfaction of doing something useful with my hands while I muddled through these uncertain times.

I strived to master the "knit one, purl two" primer. Apparently, my mother had learned to knit from her paternal grandmother, who was Austrian born. She knit in the European fashion. Not knowing the American way, I had no basis for comparison. At first, I struggled with holding the needles and the yarn, digging through a stitch here, dropping one there, while trying to maintain a tension that would provide even rows of stitches. Through exasperated sighs that I can still hear to this day, my mother had me undo the rows and start again, until I had finally managed a six-inch square that showed some promise. Mother assured me, although she confessed to not knowing anything more than the rudiments of knitting, that I could follow any pattern once I had learned these two stitches. She was right—I could.

I returned to school, simple sweater pattern and wool in hand. I felt the healing influence of working the lush blue-green wool into something lovely and comprehensible. I could create something concrete in the midst of destruction. My friends stared at me as I took out my wares and began knitting. Thinking they were impressed with the fact that I had left on vacation knowing nothing of knitting and had returned with knowledge and a plan, I smiled proudly. Then one said quite bluntly, "You're knitting backwards." They all laughed then. "It's not backwards, it's European," I replied. It took them a while to concede.

Alas, I am no great knitter. I was then and am now a fairly adept fumbler when armed with needles and yarn. I lack the creativity to compose the harmonious symphony of colors and textures implicit in any definition of an accomplished artisan. I'm intimidated by a blank, whether it is a clean piece of paper, a canvas, or simply an unknown. I have no trouble envisioning a finished product, but technically figuring out the "how" of something defeats me. However, this has not deterred me from plugging along, oblivious to the fact that all too frequently I have to undo what has taken me hours to do. It probably takes me four times longer to make something than it does anyone else on the planet. I don't believe I ever finished that first sweater I started so long ago.

I went on to finish school, though, to marry and become a mother myself. In my very traditional world, women tended to knit layettes when expecting babies. When I was pregnant, I felt as though I should knit something, too, so not knowing whether I was carrying a boy or a girl, I made a mint-green sweater and hat. Later, I also tried my hand at crocheting, embroidery, needlepoint, and sewing, only to return chastened and resigned to the mother of needlework, knitting.

Knitting is portable. It doesn't take up an inordinate amount of space and it doesn't tax my failing vision. Striped pullovers and cardigans with sailboats taken from French knitting-pattern books for children, then Irish-knit sweaters, mittens, socks, and cabled gloves for my brother spewed from my hands. The more intricate the pattern, the more concentration it took, the better I liked it and the more apt I was to complete it. Perhaps I'm just perverse by nature, but every pattern I'm drawn to is of complex design. One of my favorites was the navy blue children's cardigan with row after row of tiny red boats with white sails.

As I began in knitting, so have I endured. I knit when I've got something on my mind. It need not be of a negative nature, only something in need of serious attention. There were literally years when I knit nothing, absolutely nothing. I didn't miss it. The years when I knit nothing were the years when I had found a substitute in sewing, calligraphy, or painting, although I didn't like the results of crocheting and didn't need or want any calligraphy embellishing my walls. But I've realized in the past several years that I knit as a meditation and a comfort. It's what gets me through the hurdles of chaos. There have been few times in my life that had a shortage of subjects for contemplation (return to school, moves, switching jobs, and issues with more profound psychological and spiritual effects), and consequently, no lack of knitting projects. I'm no longer sure whether I reach my decisions while engrossed in the meditation of knitting, or whether I'm simply freeing my space and forbidding entry to those who would have the audacity to interrupt my quietude. I can relate this feeling to times as a child when I had found something to absorb me totally—a book, a school report, drawing, or playing the piano—only to be summoned by my mother to immediately perform some menial task. This frequently triggered a boiling rage in me; it showed that another person could not and would not respect my space. I erected walls of resistance that have carried over to my present life.

Almost nothing could have been more chaotic than my life in 1999 when my mother fell and broke her hip. My husband and I, having just returned from a six month cruising sabbatical on our beloved sailboat, had settled into a new home, in a new city, and into new jobs. But family comes first, and my job could be put on hold. My mother had already been diagnosed with a life-threatening illness and with a broken hip, she would need all the courage and determination she could muster to survive. Taking care of the dying is what I went to nursing school for, and it is what I have lovingly and at times passionately done for twenty-five years. Dying is my life. Taking care of my dying mother was another story. To say that Mother did not recuperate gracefully is an understatement, given her low tolerance for dependence on others. For six-and-a-half months she was cantankerous and uncooperative. As a hospice nurse, I had often found myself an advisor and confidante to patients and families; bonds often form in the intimacy of the dying process. But instead of seeking my opinions or accepting my support, my mother steadily constructed a fragile but impenetrable shell around her, letting nothing and no one in. But through the porous shell seeped her vulnerability and anguish. Reaching out to her was rewarded only by silence and later, rage. Between puffs of oxygen, she inhaled gulps of cigarette smoke as if her life depended not on the oxygen, but on the nicotine. In the first months, I shopped and cooked for her, trying to coax something nutritious and tasty into her, but she preferred whiskey and tobacco to food. The physical therapist and I encouraged her to walk as much as possible, but she seemed disinterested for the most part. She showed no appreciation for the fact that my husband was 1,400 miles away working while I was caring for her. She ranted about everything and everyone. I was frustrated and angry. Frustrated because Mother had begged me to stay and care for her so that she didn't have to have a stranger with her and angry because I suddenly had no control over my life. She raged, and I sought some form of diversion so that I could go on being there for her. The solution came to me in a flash. I got myself some yarn at the local knitting shop and began to knit.

Mother then had a stroke and was both inconsolable and uncontrollable in her frustration. Mother fumed and raged. I knit. On and on I knitted. When she was bedridden and unresponsive, I knit and pondered life, us, and anything else that presented itself. I sat in a chair by her bed, abandoning the precious yarn only to take care of her basic needs and mine. I was running out of time to reach any kind of armistice with my mother, and my world was ugly and painful. The years of social, political, and spiritual disagreement between us had grown over time from silence to a cautious and limited list of safe subjects: the weather, our gardens, perhaps a recipe. There were things I wanted to say now, things I wanted her to know. My despair, punctuated with tears, grew by the day. I needed to create something life sustaining, something that would reach beyond the anguish around me.

Each stitch brought me closer to the creation of my fantasy of wholeness and beauty. Before too long, I was unable to decipher fact from fancy, and as the days wore on my meditation grew deeper and more humble. The stitches were imbued with colors: the rosiness of love, the quiet green of healing, and the blue of vast seas. I examined my life as my mother's ebbed away. We weren't much alike, were we? Then why when I looked in the mirror did I see her? She had given up on me at an early age, yet I was there caring for her as one would an infant, and I couldn't imagine not doing so. The times when I contemplated leaving her were ground away by a fearsome force drawing me back to my self-inflicted role of nurturer. I needed to give that which I had not received; incomprehensibly, I needed to be caretaker to my mother.

My mother lay in a hospital bed in her living room with a view of her precious garden, which retained its loveliness even in early September. Vases of flowers adorned nearby tables, all within her line of sight should she awaken. A vague scent of lavender lingered on the linens, and a lone candle burned on the mantle. There was a quiet beyond that of earth. In that quiet my mother's last breath was barely audible. I held her hand as she left this world, and when at last I looked down at the completed knitting in my lap, I fully expected to see the rainbow of color my imagination had created, and within that landscape, a rich tapestry of truth, beauty, and love. There instead lay a black shawl—I had imagined it all. What hadn't been my imagination, though, was that each stitch I had knitted contained a particle of my love, not only for my mother, but for my daughter, my brother, my husband, and my friends past and present.

In the first hours after my mother died, I bathed her withered body, scarcely more than a skeleton even then, as I had bathed so many others. Finding a colorful dress, I slipped it over her head, pulled it down, and tucked it around her, folding her hands over her heart when I was done. I brushed her hair and placed in it, one on either side, two pansy clips my daughter had brought her. I sat down beside her bed, waiting for the undertaker, and at last I asked her why she didn't like me. I thought I heard her reply that she never understood. Then I imagined that she told me that she herself, from the time she was a tiny girl, had never felt loved, and so had never learned to love herself or to show affection to the children she brought into this world. "Don't you know," I answered, "that we loved you in spite of everything? Don't you know that when the threads of life are woven together to form a pattern of interdependence, there is no choice but to love?"

Days later, in the attic among my mother's belongings, I weeded through long-forgotten pieces of personal history: letters with foreign stamps, Belgian lace handkerchiefs, dried red roses—all obviously once cherished for what will now always be unknown memories. I took my time slipping off faded ribbons and opening crumbling papers in an attempt to put together the life of the person I had known for fifty-five years, a person I scarcely understood and of whose own childhood there is not a single photograph or memento. My mother eluded me much as a cat fading into the shadows eludes its prey. Then one afternoon, hidden in numerous caches throughout her downstairs rooms, I found stashes of chocolate from a previous life of indulgence. Obviously, there was one thing we shared—our chocolate fetish. At that precise minute, from some recess of the house, I heard my mother's laughter.

Eventually, I came across the moth-eaten remains of a tangerine-colored sweater, wrapped in yellowing tissue paper and tucked away on a shelf in the back of her cedar closet. Stitches still clung to a pair of silver needles, as though the knitter had every intention of returning to complete the project. Multiple holes invaded the fabric, verifying that at least some critters had made use of the sweater's warmth. The sweater symbolized so many things. It felt to me as though my mother had put our relationship on the shelf along with that sweater, and that, like that sweater, it had become tattered and worn. It seemed that by relegating it to a closet shelf, there was no hope of a resurrection or a mending of the threads of our broken lives.

I wondered so many things. Why had my mother begun the sweater in the first place? Why had she never finished it? Had the sweater been intended for me, as I had once so wished? Had I not proven myself worthy of it? And, I wondered, why did my mother knit? The reason I keep knitting isn't because I'm obsessed with a project or in need of a garment or a gift, although assuredly that is a benefit. Knitting is an excuse to block out the world and at the same time come to terms with my feelings about it: to sift and discard, to unravel and rewind endless strands of time. Knitting is a mystical train ride into a sacred territory, awaiting discovery from within. Did my mother knit to find answers? Had she given it up because it was too painful to find those answers? I'll never know. I do know that since her death I have not knit a single black thing.

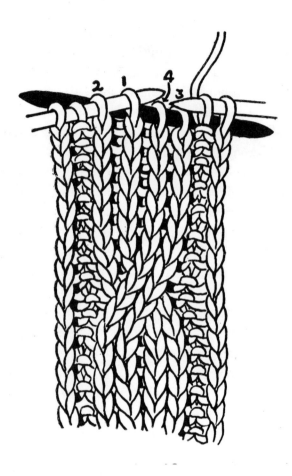

Book Resources

Books about knitting abound, of course. Below is but a small selection, written by contributors to this volume; mentioned by them in their essays; or inspired by their themes. It is by no means comprehensive or encompassing. Two good resources for buying knitting titles online are needleartsbookshop.com and schoolhousepress.com. Knittersreview.com runs a helpful review column on knitting-related books.

BOOKS BY CONTRIBUTORS

Chin, Lily M. *Mosaic Magic: Afghans Made Easy*. Des Moines: Oxmoor House, 1999.

———. *Knit and Crochet with Beads*. Loveland, CO: Interweave Press, 2004.

———. *The Urban Knitter*. New York: Berkley Trade, 2002.

Christiansen, Betty. *Knitting for Peace*. New York: Stewart, Tabori & Chang, 2006.

Durham, Teva. *Loop-d-Loop: More than 40 Novel Designs for Knitters*. New York: Stewart, Tabori & Chang, 2005.

Lynn, Elanor. *Country Living Cozy Knits for Cuddly Babies*. New York: Hearst, 2006.

Nargi, Lela. *Knitting Lessons: Tales from the Knitting Path*. New York: Tarcher/Penguin, 2003.

BOOKS MENTIONED IN THIS VOLUME

Bliss, Debbie. *New Baby Knits: More Than 30 Patterns for 0–3 Year Olds*. New York: St. Martin's Press, 1991.

Fanderl, Lisl. *Bäuerliches Stricken 1–3*. Rosenheim, Germany: Rosenheimer Verlagshaus, 2001.

Lattimore, Richmond, translator. *The Odyssey of Homer*. New York: Harper Perennial Modern Classics, 1999.

Thompson, Gladys. *Patterns for Guernseys, Jerseys and Arans: Fishermen's Sweaters from the British Isles, third revised edition*. New York: Dover Publications, 1971.

Walker, Barbara G. *A Treasury of Knitting Patterns.* Pittsville, WI: Schoolhouse Press, 1998.

Walker, Barbara G. *A Second Treasury of Knitting Patterns*. Pittsville, WI: Schoolhouse Press, 1998.

Walker, Barbara G. *Charted Knitting Designs: A Third Treasury of Knitting Patterns.* Pittsville, WI: Schoolhouse Press, 1998.

Walker, Barbara G. *A Fourth Treasury of Knitting Patterns.* Pittsville, WI: Schoolhouse Press, 2000.

BOOKS ON THEMES
Bons Mots

Dregni, Michael, editor. *Knitticisms . . . And Other Purls of Wisdom.* Stillwater, MN: Voyageur Press, 2005.

Cornell, Kari, editor. *Knitting Yarns and Spinning Tales: A Knitter's Stash of Wit and Wisdom.* Stillwater, MN: Voyageur Press, 2005.

Pearl-McPhee, Stephanie. *At Knit's End: Meditations for Women Who Knit Too Much.* North Adams, MA: Storey Publishing, 2005.

Roghaar, Linda, and Molly Wolf, (Eds.). *KnitLit the Third: We Spin More Yarns.* New York: Three Rivers Press, 2005.

Dyeing

Buchanan, Rita. *A Dyer's Garden: From Plant to Pot: Growing Dyes for Natural Fibers*. Loveland, CO: Interweave Press, 1995.

Eskesen, Elaine. *Dyeing to Knit: How to Use—and Create—Your Own Beautiful Hand-dyed Yarns*. Rockport, ME: Down East Books, 2005.

Klos, Dagmar. *The Dyer's Companion*. Loveland, CO: Interweave Press, 2005.

Lesch, Alma. *Vegetable Dyeing: 151 Color Recipes for Dyeing Yarns and Fabrics with Natural Materials*. New York: Watson-Guptill, 1971.

Potter, Cheryl. *Handpaint Country*. Sioux Falls, SD: XRX Books, 2002.

Finishing

Crowfoot, Jane. *All Stitched Up*. Hauppauge, NY: Barron's Educational Series, 2003.

Epstein, Nicky. *Knitting Over the Edge: Unique Ribs, Cords, Appliqués, Color, Eclectic—The Second Essential Collection of*

Decorative Borders. New York: Sixth & Spring Books, 2005.

Wiseman, Nancie M. *The Knitter's Book of Finishing Techniques.* Woodinville, WA: Martingale & Company, 2002.

Gardens

Messent, Jan. *Knitted Gardens.* Petaluma, CA: Search Press, 1992.

History

Macdonald, Anne L. *No Idle Hands: The Social History of American Knitting.* New York: Ballantine Books, 1990.

Rutt, Richard. *History of Hand Knitting.* Loveland, CO: Interweave Press, 2003.

Leftovers

Albright, Barbara. *Odd Ball Knitting: Creative Ideas for Leftover Yarn.* New York: Clarkson Potter, 2005.

Melville, Sally. *Styles.* Sioux Falls, SD: XRX Books, 2002.

Messent, Jan. *Have You Any Wool? The Creative Use of Yarn*. Petaluma, CA: Search Press, 1993.

Mending

Barnes, Mary Galpin, (Ed.). *Knitting Tips and Trade Secrets: Clever Solutions for Better Hand Knitting, Machine Knitting, and Crocheting*. Newtown, CT: Taunton Press, 1996.

Columbo, Toni. *How to Fix Holes in Sweaters: The 8 Simple Secrets of Invisible Re-Knitting*. Hayes Service Group Inc., 1993.

Righetti, Maggie. *Knitting in Plain English*. New York: St. Martin's Griffin, 1986.

Zimmermann, Elizabeth. *Elizabeth Zimmermann's Knitting Workshop*. Pittsville, WI: Schoolhouse Press, 1981.

Off the Grid

New, Debbie. *Unexpected Knitting*. Pittsville, WI: Schoolhouse Press, 2003.

Zilboorg, Anna. *Knitting for Anarchists*. Petaluma, CA: Unicorn Books for Craftsmen, 2002.

Patchwork

Abrahams, Debbie. *100 Afghan Squares to Knit*. North Pomfret, VT: Trafalgar Square Publishing, 2002.

Selfridge, Gail. *Patchwork Knitting*. New York: Watson-Guptill, 1977.

Pattern Making

Budd, Ann. *The Knitter's Handy Book of Sweater Patterns: Basic Designs in Multiple Sizes and Gauges*. Loveland, CO: Interweave Press, 2004.

Leapman, Melissa. *A Close-Knit Family*. Newtown, CT: Taunton Press, 1999.

Thomas, Mary. *Mary Thomas's Book of Knitting Patterns*. New York: Dover Publications, 1972.

Morse, Pat. *Charting: How to Design Your Own Knitting Patterns*. P. Morse, 1985.

Spinning

Fournier, Jane, and Nola Fournier. *In Sheep's Clothing: A Handspinner's Guide to Wool.* Loveland, CO: Interweave Press, 2003.

Kroll, Carol. *The Whole Craft of Spinning: From the Raw Material to the Finished Yarn.* New York: Dover Publications, 1981.

Raven, Lee. *Hands on Spinning.* Loveland, CO: Interweave Press, 1987.

Stitch Patterns

McGregor, Sheila. *Traditional Fair Isle Knitting.* New York: Dover Publications, 2003.

Mountford, Debra, editor. *Aran and Fair Isle Knitting: Patterns, Techniques, and Stitches.* London: Collins & Brown, 2000.

Norbury, James. *Traditional Knitting Patterns from Scandinavia, the British Isles, France, Italy.* New York: Dover Publications, 1973.

Waller, Jane. *Classic Knitting Patterns from the British Isles: Men's Hand-Knits from the 20's to the 50's.* London: Thames and Hudson, 1985.

Walker, Barbara G. *The Craft of Cable-Stitch Knitting.* New York: Scribner, 1971.

Traditional Knits

Gibson-Roberts, Priscilla A. *Knitting in the Old Way: Designs and Techniques from Ethnic Sweaters.* White River Junction, VT: Nomad Press, 2004.

Hartley, Marie, and Joan Ingilby. *The Old Hand Knitters of the Dales: With an Introduction to the Early History of Knitting.* North Yorkshire, U.K.: Dalesman Publishing Company Ltd., 1991.

NOTES ON THE CONTRIBUTORS

Born in 1944 and raised in New York City, **Veda Alban** is a hospice-care nurse in Port Charlotte, Florida. She contributes articles on end-of-life care to Lippincott Williams and Wilkins medical publishers, and is a mental-health volunteer for the American Red Cross in disaster relief services. She is married and is the mother of one grown daughter; she is also grandmother to one granddaughter.

Kathryn Alexander is a handspinner, weaver, and knitter who uses only her own handspun singles yarns for her work. Kathryn uses her ability to make yarns as the focus of all her cloth. Using this knowledge of how yarns are made lets her manipulate the surface of woven and knit fabric, turning the physics of yarn into the main element of her designs. She lives in upstate New York, where she gardens and rides her horses when she is not working in her studio, which over looks rolling hay fields rimmed with hard woods, to the background noise of crickets, wild turkeys, and spring peepers.

Eiko Berkowitz was born in Tokyo, Japan, and moved to New York City in 1985. She now owns the store YU on the

218

Lower East Side, which sells new and pre-owned collectable Japanese designer clothing. She also designs her own clothing, works on knitting (every aspect including shearing, dyeing, spinning, knitting, felting, and weaving), and makes her own line of handmade soaps that feature Golden Silk from Japan. When she is not busy doing all of this, she is playing with her nine cats and wearing one of her 900+ (Amy Downs) hats.

Jennifer Brown lives and knits in rural central Vermont. Between running her business, Opaque Design & Print Production, with her husband, and wrangling her infant daughter, two dogs, and three cats, she's trying like mad to find more time to work on her own writing. This book marks the first time her writing has appeared in something other than the newspaper.

Cedric N. Chatterley was born in Massena, New York, in 1956. His work has been supported by the National Endowment for the Arts and by state arts and humanities agencies in Illinois, Maine, North Carolina, and South Dakota. Most recently, he collaborated with Barbara Lau and Chris Nesbitt to produce a book for young readers: Sokita Celebrates the New Year—A Cambodian American Holiday. Published by the Greensboro Historical Museum, this book is part of a major exhibit based on the Cambodian-American community in Greensboro, North Carolina. It won the Multicultural Children's Book Award from the National Association for Multicultural Education, 2004.

Born and reared in New York City, **Lily M. Chin** has designed professionally since junior high school. Her classes and workshops are in great demand around the country. She is the author of numerous books on knitting and crocheting. She has won a few international contests and has been named the World's Fastest Crocheter. Since 2002, Lily has made over fifty television appearances and has been cited in countless newspapers and magazines, both national and international, not to mention radio interviews. Her designs have graced the pages of the very familiar knitting and crochet magazines. She is the first American designer with her name on a branded yarn label. View the Lily Chin Signature Collection at www.lilychinsignaturecollection.com.

Betty Christiansen knits and writes in La Crosse, Wisconsin, where she lives with her husband. She is the author of *Knitting for Peace* (Stewart, Tabori & Chang, 2006), and her writing has appeared in several knitting magazines, as well as *Knitting Yarns and Spinning Tales* (Voyageur Press, 2005), *For the Love of Knitting* (Voyageur Press, 2004), and *KnitLit (too)* (Three Rivers Press, 2004).

Robert Bruce Cowan holds a Ph.D. in comparative literature from the Graduate Center of the City University of New York. While he doesn't knit himself, he considers himself an expert spectator of knitting.

Teva Durham is the author of *Loop-d-Loop: More Than 40 Novel Designs for Knitters* (Stewart, Tabori & Chang, 2005). Her designs and articles are featured in top knitting magazines and numerous books, including Melanie Falick's *Handknit Holidays* and *Weekend Knitting* (Stewart, Tabori & Chang), Pam Allen's *Wrap Style* and *Scarf Style* (Interweave Press), and, *For the Love of Knitting* and *Spinning Yarns and Telling Tales* (Voyageur Press). She is currently working on a book of crochet designs. A perpetual student of life, Teva (pronounced with a soft e) brings a unique perspective to her craft. Trained as an actress and a writer, she worked as a fashion reporter and trend forecaster before giving herself over to her "hobby." She launched loop-d-loop.com, featuring her innovative line of hand knits, in 2000. She has taught knitting at yarn shops as well as New York's premier holistic institute, the Open Center.

Caroline Herzog moved from Innsbruck, Austria, to the United States in 1983. She now lives with her husband, two children, and a dog in the foothills of the Green Mountains. She owns a knitting shop, the Vermont Yarn Company, in Middlebury, Vermont.

Reine Wing Hewitt is a Brooklyn-based knitter and bookmaker. She received a bachelor's degree in book arts and experimental writing from Hampshire College. Reine teaches nontraditional and process-oriented bookmaking and knitting. She is never without a knitting project and usually has five or six going at once.

Elanor Lynn has been knitting since 1974. She is the founder of Purls of Hope, a volunteer knitting program at Children's Hope Foundation that benefits families living with HIV and AIDS in New York City. Her love of knitting and of making original garments, housewares, and other objects has inspired her to teach hundreds of knitters. Elanor grew up on in a rural, spiritual community in Vermont, and after a brief stay in New York in 1985, she studied choreography, anthropology, architecture, and painting at Bennington College. Her current knitting is inspired by natural forms, including trees, flowers, fish, water, and snakes, combined with abstract cubism in the crazy-quilt tradition. Elanor specializes in teaching make-it-up-as-you-go techniques, top-down seamless sweaters, and improvisational knitting. She lives in

Brooklyn, and her first book is *Country Living Cozy Knits for Cuddly Babies* (Sterling, 2006). She can be reached at elanorknits@yahoo.com.

Diane Mennella resides in Manhattan and knits wherever she is. She has taught knitting in yarn shops in Brooklyn and Manhattan over the last ten years, has been a member of the Big Apple Knitters guild practically since its inception, and looks forward to the next technological breakthrough that will make the days long enough to engage in all her passions equally. Her passions include her family, reading, piano four-hand playing, shape-note singing, and, last but certainly not least, knitting.

Lela Nargi is a knitter, author, former journalist, and recent transplant from New York City to rural Vermont. Her book *Knitting Lessons: Tales from the Knitting Path* (Tarcher/Penguin, 2003) documented her adventures in learning to knit, and also featured dozens of interviews with knitters around the country, as a means to understanding what it is about the practice of knitting that draws people in and keeps them returning, sometimes obsessively, to their yarn. A recent essay about knitting, "Knitting Is Work and the Widows of Sant'Arsenio" is included in *Knitting Yarns and Spinning Tales*, (Voyageur Press, 2005), edited by Kari Cornell.

Her literary nonfiction work—most of it related to memoir, travel, and food—appears in numerous national and international magazines and journals. *Around the Table: Women on Food, Cooking, Nourishment, Love . . . and the Mothers Who Dished It Up for Them* was released by Tarcher/Penguin in 2005. Find her at www.lelanargi.com.

Still living in that drafty farmhouse on the coast of Maine, **Clara Parkes** achieves her yarnirvana by writing about yarn for *Knitter's Review*. Nonknitting time is spent spinning, dyeing, gardening, drinking far too much tea, and dreaming of projects to come. You can read her insights and discoveries at www.knittersreview.com.

Lydia Vivante works at a contemporary art museum in Long Island City, New York. She divides her time between New York City and Wellfleet, Massachusetts.